The
Leadership
of Worship

The Leadership of Worship

GRADY HARDIN

with illustrations by Bruce A. Sayre

Abingdon

Nashville

The
Leadership
of Worship

Copyright © 1980 by Abingdon

Library of Congress Cataloging in Publication Data

HARDIN, H. GRADY.
  The leadership of worship.
  Includes bibliographical references.
  1. Public worship. I. Title.
  BV15.H37   264   79-26863

ISBN 0-687-21160-3

MANUFACTURED BY THE PARTHENON PRESS AT
NASHVILLE, TENNESSEE, UNITED STATES OF AMERICA

CONTENTS

63020

PREFACE

The meaning of any spoken word is filtered through a complex combination of many components: the accepted definition of the word itself, the tone of voice used in speaking, the facial expressions and bodily motions accompanying the sound, and the whole context of time and place. Separating any one part of the expression from any other part is difficult; yet understanding the significance of the meaning lies in being alert to the way in which each part of communication influences the whole. A Christian congregation at worship combines intentions and beliefs to express in commonly accepted ways its response to God's gift of life through Jesus Christ. To know *why* we worship is of prime importance. Theological reasons for worship and the ways in which worship is accomplished are inseparable in the sense that the *why* depends on the *how*, yet the *how* is subordinate to the *why*. In order that the worship of churches may be faithful and effective, we will be concerned here with the ways we worship and how worship services are led; therefore, we might say we are turning our attention to important secondary matters.

In every worship service an underlying theology is evident, but my own theological convictions are not presented here in any systematic way. I hope the suggestions made about leading worship will be of value to those who hold different theological convictions; however, there is no sense in which I have tried to avoid the influence of my own personal faith, if indeed, that could be possible.

Should anyone get the impression that I am presenting *the* way to lead worship, my intention will have been misunderstood or I have failed to make my intention clear. There may be a specific way that a particular person should lead an act of worship, but we normally can assume that there is no *one* way that worship should be conducted.

There will be little use of the terms traditional, innovative, or experimental worship here. The relationship of these words to worship is so inexact that I cannot use them with clarity. Also, emotional overtones distort our reactions to them. For instance, "innovative" or "experimental" worship has begun to conjure up pictures of contrived forms that ignore the essential purposes of worship. This reaction has led many to cling to a "traditionalism" based on no more than repetition.

My intention is to discuss many choices in ways of leading worship in order to enable members of the congregation to participate more fully. For many congregations this active involvement will be an innovation, to rediscover the tradition of worship as liturgy—that is, the work of the people. The conduct of worship by an effective leader is not in itself the worship of the congregation. The whole congregation's being led to participate in the prayers and praise and proclamations and offerings is the radical change demanded. The word radical is used to speak of the revitalization of the root system of the people's worship. Familiarity with our heritage will be an important guide as new ways and patterns are tried.

There is a hunger to hear the Word of God, to reenact our being made God's people, and to respond to this gift of life in thanksgiving. This work of the people must have ground rules and leadership—important secondary considerations that make the liturgy possible. The importance of the role of the leader cannot be exaggerated. The church selects someone to announce, "The Lord is risen!" The way in which this is spoken leads the congregation to respond, "The Lord is risen indeed!" This exchange is, in sum, what this book is about.

Important secondary matters retain their proper place so long as the leader is clear about the priorities. Such a statement is so much easier to say than to do. To be the one to say "The Lord is risen" in the midst of the church gathered for worship is to suggest a theology of the church and its ordained ministry. The person who leads worship must be fully grounded in such primary matters in order to fulfill the important secondary matters. There should always be a tension within the leader between person and office. The ordained representative of the church is chosen, trained, and authorized to say "The Lord is risen," but this representative is always a person with varieties of gifts, graces, weaknesses, all wrapped up in the uniqueness of a personality. In ordaining persons the church takes the same risks God does in using folks to reveal God's truth.

The ordained should become a representative person in conducting worship in order to be a means of God's grace. The rub comes when the resurrection faith which calls for dying to the old self and rising as a new person is subverted by the propensity for self-preservation. The leader can speak out boldly because the gospel is true, even though the bold move is accompanied by the prayer, "Lord, have mercy"—and God does!

Categories of worship leadership are arranged in several ways. I have chosen to examine leadership in terms of those with whom we work, what is said, what is done, things used, clothes worn, and how time is spent. Leadership in specific services includes all the above categories; and, therefore, I have not discussed the "how to" of different services as a chapter by itself.

My original intention was to present these categories in an ecumenical manner, but I soon became aware of the difficulties of discussing worship leadership outside a denominational stance. Since there is not *a* way Methodists conduct services of worship, I hope my Methodist identity will add perspective without serious limitations.

I received direct assistance on an early revision of this manuscript from colleagues who read carefully and made helpful suggestions. All their suggestions were taken seriously, some of them were followed precisely, others helped me reexamine my presentation. I withstood the temptation to write their book, so it is my book made better by their generous help. The Assistant General Secretary, Section on Worship of the Board of Discipleship of The United

Methodist Church, Hoyt Hickman, made helpful comments. William S. Babcock, church historian and colleague, knows how to use and punctuate the English language and has helped me mightily to do the same. James F. White, faculty colleague and liturgical scholar, not only read and commented on this manuscript but has been an integral part of my own growth as a leader of worship. Fred Kandeler read with meticulous care. He is one of those gifted persons with whom I have led many services and never collided. He helped because he knew what I intended to say even when I was not saying it. Joseph D. Quillian, Jr., my dean, read and marked the manuscript with care, wrote careful notes, and spent a considerable block of time in discussion. Joe Quillian was being much more than dean, he was being the Professor of Preaching and Worship he is but has little opportunity to practice. His influence on me and this book is profound. Bruce Arthur Sayre is an artist, pastor, former student, and friend. In this book he and I are saying something together. Our work has helped my work. Mary Ann Marshall, who typed the manuscript skillfully, has dealt with me with patience and good will; for this I am grateful.

Rowena Hardin has read each revision of the manuscript. More than that, I cannot think of myself as a leader of worship or as a person without thinking of her influence on our life together.

The
Leadership
of Worship

ONE

The Planning Team

In *The Book of Worship*[1]
of The United Methodist Church published in 1964
the title "The Order of Worship" is used to
designate the regular order of service. The book
which this one replaced, published in 1944, had
suggested a large number of orders of worship. The
definite article probably had not been used with an
order of worship for a regular Sunday service
(without Holy Communion) since John Wesley
sent over *The Sunday Service* to the American
Methodists in 1784. The reaction of Methodists in
both centuries was very much alike: the service
was not widely used. Ministers simply did not take
the order, or suggestion, seriously. This may be
difficult for Episcopalians or Lutherans or Roman
Catholics to understand, but the Free Church
tradition, in which Methodism has had at least one
foot, has always been wary of orders of worship so
fixed that the freedom of the leader might be
abridged. Interestingly enough, if one were to
attend a very "free" congregation for a month, the
order would probably turn out to be virtually
invariable; at least a fixed pattern would begin to
show. In United Methodist congregations today the
usual orders of worship reflect local tradition to
some extent, but they also reflect even more the

15

patterns preferred by the pastors in charge at the time. Most members are willing to leave to the current pastor the order of worship he or she plans. Some concern may be expressed when a radical change is made from the forms used by a beloved predecessor, or when some favorite hymns or songs are never used; but usually there is a that's-what-we-are-paying-you-for attitude toward the order of worship a particular minister uses.

Since 1964 many churches and denominations

have studied their orders of worship and have produced new services and service books. The United Methodist Church has been a part of this vigorous liturgical ferment. The 1972 General Conference authorized the preparation of alternate forms of worship by the Section on Worship of the Board of Discipleship. An alternate text for the Eucharist was printed in 1972, and the service was used at the meeting of the General Conference that year.[2] The Section on Worship produced an alternate service for Baptism, Confirmation, and Renewal in 1976 with a less spectacular, but brisk sale. In the same year *Word and Table: A Basic Pattern of Sunday Worship for United Methodists*[3] presented a pattern for worship very close to the pattern of the alternate Communion service of 1972 with a commentary, an alternate lectionary, and translations of our traditional creeds, prayers, and canticles prepared by the International Consultation on English Texts.

As this book is being written, the Section on Worship is completing work on alternate texts for weddings and funerals. There will be a revised form of *Word and Table* under another title. The ferment will continue, and it should be many years before services are fixed. It is safe to say, however, that it is not likely that there will ever be another service that claims to be *the* order. On any given Sunday the bulletin of a congregation will outline *the* order of worship. It is my recommendation that such an order be prepared by a planning team chaired by the pastor with representatives from the congregation. Where there is a ministerial staff, they might be included. This obvious point is made because so many services of worship are not the result of conscious planning. Unfortunately, some services are unified only at the desk of the secretary who types the copy for the bulletin. In many churches where the pastor is also the secretary, some broader planning can take place if the minister-typist and choir director inform each other of their plans for Sunday. Those of us who have been in this position know how inadequate such planning usually is—however, it's a start.

Planning for worship with a team of concerned and representative persons is not an activity many ministers have experienced regularly. Few congregations or ministers are demanding it, even though such planning can be a means of more vital worship and church life.

Most ministers know and have experienced the advantages of planning in services where planning has long been taken for granted. A funeral demands planning. The minister in charge, the family of the deceased, the funeral director, and the musicians must plan together. There may not be meetings of all these persons for each individual service, but every minister should have a meeting with the funeral directors in the community early in the pastorate to discuss funerals in general. First of all, this can be an important meeting for those people who will work together often under a variety of circumstances. There ought to be clear understandings of the responsibilities of each person. What are the local customs well established in the community for the reverent burial of a body? What types of services are usually conducted? What music has been considered appropriate? How has the time and location of the service usually been set? A pastor need only be in one funeral where planning is inadequate and the actions of others unexpected, surprising, or conflicting to discover the absolute necessity of advance planning. In some situations, even when the best of planning has taken place, there may still be some confusion, but confusion can be faced best by leaders who know and understand each other and the framework within which they will operate.

A wedding is a service where many powerful forces meet. The minister in charge of the service can coordinate these forces by good planning or be caught in the vortex of engulfing powers. In formal weddings in the church a complex set of demands converge. Each congregation should have a well-established set of guidelines to encourage the use of the church for weddings (and funerals) by members. If such guidelines have never been adopted it can be awkward to try to make a drastic change in a particular service. Whether a change will be drastic or not depends on whose prerogatives have been invaded. Just announce that flowers may be placed here but not there and you discover how badly advance planning is needed.

The pastor (or guest minister), the church musician (or the musician brought in), the florist, the wedding consultant, the bride and her family, the groom and his family, and often others must help plan the service. Ask anyone who has participated in as many as ten weddings to give an account of the most memorable one, and the need for good planning will be obvious. Respect for each other, a belief in the importance of marriage and this particular union, an awareness of the importance of each desire of every person involved, will call for the best pastoral skills from the minister in charge of the service.

The role of the clergy to initiate planning for weddings and funerals touches one's whole ministry. The entire pastoral office will be called upon in these liturgical responsibilities. Occasionally ministers find themselves in situations where they are called on to function only in the service itself with little planning. But this should be unusual. One ought to go into any service with at least some knowledge of who is expected to do what and when and where. One's ministry can be of service when the whole ministerial team cooperates to make the service of worship a glorification of God and a ministry to a congregation and particular members of it at a significant moment of their lives.

If planning for worship is important for weddings and funerals—as well as anniversaries, dedications, recognitions, and other special services—it is certainly important for the principal gathering of the congregation on Sunday. Most ministers will agree about that need. Yet the minister, who is most likely to be in a position to establish a pattern for planning, is the very one who doesn't plan events. If you are a minister who has not established a planning procedure, perhaps it would be helpful to give yourself permission not to start some heroic effort but only a small beginning. It may be penitential enough just to start by meeting with the person who is in charge of the music! Most often the church musician is the one who calls for advance planning and keenly feels the need for it. There are many different sizes of churches and staffs, but no matter what the size of the congregation, there is probably someone in the service who plays a musical instrument or in some way leads or assists people in singing. The minister and the musician together can form the team.

What is the agenda of the meeting? The agenda can be the music of the service or any other mutual concern. The real value of the meeting will be the opportunity for two people responsible for worship in the church to begin to broaden their base of concern and coordination. A situation in which this begins to happen in an informal way may soon turn into regular planning and discussions of the theology of worship between pastor and choir director. It can then move into a weekly meeting between pastor and choir for a brief but important few minutes at each choir rehearsal. This is not a time for the pastor to give a seminary course to the choir. Rather, it is an opportunity for study and growth for both pastor and choir members which may result in more vital and informed worship for the whole congregation.

I had a unique opportunity to participate in a near-ideal situation, and I relate it here in the hope that it will inspire others to do what is possible in their situation. As a faculty member of a seminary, I was asked to be the minister of an alternate worship service established in a large church by a committee exploring the possibilities of such a service with the full backing of the pastor in charge and a large staff. Every possible form of encouragement and support was offered. The chapel was made available at eleven o'clock on Sunday morning. An organist-director was assigned to the service. A seminary student was employed to assist. After a year an associate minister was assigned to the service. A layperson who was well-trained in worship and the visual arts, and who had been active in the project from the start, was included.

At first we four met weekly to discuss worship, but our primary concern was to get ready for Sunday. In time a pattern emerged which represented an optimum procedure for planning. The general structure of our work included long planning meetings which would look ahead to the next season of the church year or other period of time covering at least two months. The lectionary assigned for the Sundays we were planning began to be the basis for our discussions. As chairperson and preacher I had read the lessons and jotted down any relevant ideas that were suitable for sermons or liturgical emphases. On a sheet of paper each of us listed the date, lectionary readings, Sunday of the church year, any other calendar emphasis, and service assignments.

The central importance of the lectionary should be emphasized at this point. The years in which this particular planning team worked came at a time when the Consultation on Church Union was preparing a consensus lectionary. The Roman Catholics were preparing one in the new liturgical atmosphere of post-Vatican II days; Lutherans were preparing a new lectionary and publishing preaching aids. It was our planning experience during this time of reform that the lectionary came alive for us. Not, of course, as an assignment chiseled in stone, but as a dynamic expression of the Word that is given to the church. Far from being remote from the situation in which we lived, its relevance became more obvious as we dealt with the messages of the lectionary assignments. In those years (1970–1974) the changes in lectionaries convinced me of the value of constant examination of the assignments and a willingness to change. British Methodism changes the lectionary annually and this may be too often. The three-year lectionary so widely accepted today in this country ought to be under regular observation in order to make the whole biblical message available to churches. Christians have frequently neglected the Old Testament as a source of our faith, and I regret that present lectionaries often make Old Testament assignments relate to the lessons from the four Gospels on superficial bases. (For instance, see Pentecost 5, Year B: Mark 4:35-41 and Job 38:1-11, 16-18.) But even with its weaknesses, our focus on Bible passages assigned by the lectionary was an indispensable center around which we could move.

From the dynamics of the group there began to emerge a wide variety of ideas and insights. What might start as a sermon idea could develop into some musical expression. Another tangent might lead us into an exploration of an act by the congregation that would be a means of expressing an idea. Visual possibilities began to be discussed. Most of the time the four or five of us no longer represented specific areas of worship, we became a team in which each member strengthened the others. Since each person on the team was close to the members of the congregation, our planning represented the community of worship in many ways. By the time the longer meeting ended, the worksheet for each Sunday was filled with more ideas than could ever be included in a single service.

An hour on Wednesday afternoon was then reserved to come up with the service for the Sunday after next. The need to prepare bulletin copy well in advance seemed like an undue demand placed on us by the printer, but it really helped us plan more carefully. Advance worship planning also had a salutary homiletical spillover which helped preacher and listeners. The same could be said for every other area of the service.

There was a regular examination of the orders of worship and of the means which were being used to give members of the congregation opportunities to pray and praise and respond. We found some things that worked: an original tune for the *Gloria Patri*[4] became a hallmark of the service. We found some things that did not work: processionals that move outside cannot depend on the singing ability of the congregation—they need instrumental support. Above all else, those of us who worked for two years together will be grateful for the experience. And now, years later, the effects of that planning are still felt across a wide area of United Methodism. It was this service that provided a setting for the trial use of various editions which preceded the alternate text for Holy Communion, 1972, mentioned above.

This rather brief moment of unusual worship planning did not last. The personnel changed, and other factors led members of the planning team in separate directions. Yet the experience verified the need for planning. Vital worship which involves the people and is a faithful witness and response to the Word cannot be left to one leader or to a merely acceptable order of worship. Churches do not fall into good worship practices.

Each congregation will devise its own organizational structure for its best governance. The worship of the church is often left so fully to the pastor that it is sometimes ignored when committees are established. The planning team about which I have been writing is a small, specialized group which works regularly on the ongoing worship of the congregation. There are wider concerns and involvement in worship which also should be represented in the government of the church. Music involves the choirs, the leaders, the instruments, the space. In some churches ushers are well organized and trained. To permit men and women (it will be a new discovery to some that women can usher) to usher without any training in the meaning of worship and the place of the usher in it is little short of maladministration. Acolytes and servers, and any others who have special duties during the service, are usually eager to help if they are given an understanding of their task, shown how to do it, and made to see the importance of the job in relation to the whole service.

The altar guild, or committee, has responsibility for the care of the chancel. The work of this group is vital and needs to be coordinated with all others concerned with the use of the building for worship. The use and care of the chancel is directly related to the care and storage of the equipment of the chancel. Altar cloths, vessels, hangings, candelabra, candles, vestments, and books must be used, stored, and cared for. Provision should be made by every church for adequate space and responsible persons to care for these furnishings. One ought never begin a pastorate without becoming aware of the janitorial duties that are part of the job.

There are in many congregations persons who hold no particular office whose interest in and knowledge of worship make them valuable members of the committee, or board, overseeing worship. Find these people and put them to work.

All these worship interests should be represented in a governing body with several ongoing duties: (1) to provide policies concerning the use of the church for weddings, funerals, and other services; (2) to offer occasional training programs which may include special studies in the church school and groups planning worship in general or having specific areas of interest, such as the use of music, drama, and the other arts; (3) to search for ways in which the members of the congregation will achieve full participation in worship.

A concern for worship in the whole membership can be immeasurably strengthened by one group which deals with all worship matters. A small planning team can become the executive expression of these concerns for worship.

Resources

A worship planning team can get help from many books and periodicals. Here are two magazines which are fresh with suggestions:

Nuts and Bolts of Worship, Selah Ltd., P.O. Box 632, Columbia, MD 21045. (By and for United Methodists in particular. $10 annually.)

Liturgy, The Liturgical Conference, 810 Rhode Island Avenue, N.E., Washington, D.C. 20018. (This conference is ecumenical, though chiefly Roman Catholic. Membership is $25, which includes *Liturgy.*)

TWO

Spoken Words

Do you remember the old grammar school dodge to a teacher's question—"I know the answer, but I just can't say it"? Some of us have not yet learned that we don't know something until we can articulate it. Of course, saying is not all of knowing, and certainly not all of communicating in worship. No amount of bread or possible use of it can substitute for the words, "This is my body." Tons of ink have been used to print words decrying their use! Even silent worship implies a faith known because it has been spoken.

The leader of worship uses many words. Let us examine some of the categories of these sounds.

RUBRICS

Directions for ceremonial in worship books were usually printed in red and thus were called *rubrics*, from the Latin word meaning "red." These directions must be spoken when the leader directs the people to actions and/or words. The rubric may be a call to praying or singing or standing or kneeling or any needed indication of the congregation's part in worship. The words should be chosen for their clarity and brevity, and they should be spoken in the spirit of a directive. This means that there should be no uncertainty in the congregation about what is desired, but it also means that the words should be said in such a way as to encourage people to follow the direction. Barking an order to

stand or sit may be brief and clear yet fail as an encouragement to respond. On the other hand, the uncertain sound or timid offering of a choice may result in confusion. "Let us pray" is always better than "May we pray?" The latter, as has often been said, leaves the possibility of a negative vote.

Versicles are a means the church has used for

transitions to the next part of a worship service, so they act somewhat as rubrics:

Minister: Lord, open our lips.
People: And our mouth shall proclaim your praise.
Minister: . . . Come, let us adore Him.[1]

This type rubric, which the church found helpful in its early years, has the advantage of being a clearly understood direction about what is coming next. The familiarity of these introductions makes possible the use of new acts of praise or prayers or other responses balancing the assurance of the familiar with the new. This principle is important in the planning of worship, especially when new forms are introduced.

In those congregations which are not accustomed to versicles, ministers have developed their own ways of directing congregational actions. A particularly insidious danger is that of wordy, personal ways of giving directions that call attention to the rubric itself and the leader. Asking the congregation to make an offering of money can often become more homiletical than directional. Sometimes the minister can even be suggestive of a carnival barker. Another may go to the other extreme by surprising the congregation with the appearance of ushers carrying offering plates when no word has been spoken about making an offering. Either extreme should be avoided.

The leader needs to plan the spoken rubrics with care and then practice them enough so that the congregation will get on with its worship with ease. When the leader is familiar with the material and speaks with ease, he or she may say the words with vitality and conviction without sounding unnatural.

COMMENTARY

Closely related to rubrics is what I call commentary. Most commentary by the worship leader is distracting and counterproductive. If a hymn is not a good act of praise there is no way that the leader can help by asking the congregation to "join in this act by standing and lifting hearts and voices in this glorious form that has been a part of our tradition for all these years." However, a congregation may be led to make a hymn an act of greater praise if the leader directs its attention to some particular aspect of the hymn. Selected lines of hymns may become intensely felt expressions because a pastor pointed to them with an effective commentary. A minister calling attention to the unique relation of Jesus' deeds and dreams many years ago has helped me hear a fresh message in John Hunter's "Dear Master, in Whose Life I See." An explanation to a congregation using the *Alternate Text, 1972* of why they speak the word of pardon back to the minister after the minister's pronouncement to them may be better than a whole sermon on the priesthood of all believers.

While at times these commentaries may parallel the service itself, sometimes they may be used more effectively before the service begins. Where an act of worship to be included in the order of worship is not widely familiar, it is helpful to call attention to that act and explain why it was chosen. A small congregation that had been accustomed to making its offering of money while seated with ushers distributing the plates, decided to try bringing the offerings to baskets in the chancel while the congregation sang a song printed in the bulletin. A commentary and explanation came before the service had started, and the offering experience seemed to fit into the whole service with greater ease and clearer meaning.

There may also be parts of a service which are quite familiar and which have become less meaningful partly because of their familiarity. A word about why the Lord's Prayer is used and why it is being used at a particular time may be of value occasionally. All these comments should be prepared as carefully as the program notes for a symphony concert and be as unobtrusive and helpful.

ANNOUNCEMENTS

The spoken words in a worship service triggering the most debate could well be announcements. The most unusual designation for them is probably one used in some British churches—"intimations." As one who has heard the gamut from absolutely no announcements to reading the bulletin to the congregation with embellishments, I now hold a middle position.

If a literate congregation is given a bulletin with the calendar printed therein, it ought to be encouraged to read the bulletin and depend on it for information about the time and place of meetings and other items of community concern. There may be, however, an important activity of the church which will not be noticed by the

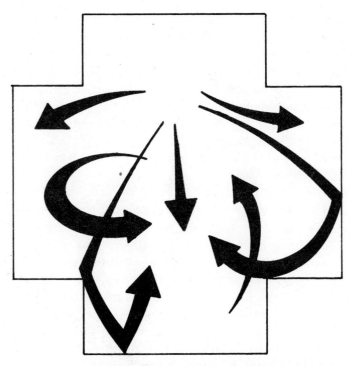

congregation unless it is brought to special
attention by a strong announcement. There should
be provided in the regular order of worship for
every congregation an opportunity to respond to
the Word of God as the community of faith it is and
may become. Among the proper responses can be
presentations of some of the activities of the church
which bear directly upon the very nature of the
congregation itself. If the room has good acoustics,
it may be helpful for persons directly related to the
activity to make the announcement. When a
member of a class tells of its project of collecting
used eyeglasses to be sent to a clinic in Haiti, the

announcement has a strong impact. Control must be exerted to ensure that these announcements are really proper concerns of the congregation which need special emphasis.

Let the planning team discuss the whole issue so that announcements can be made without hesitation or apology. If they become objectionable, change the pattern.

PRONOUNCEMENTS

The worship leader's representative role is expressed in the entire service. However, pronouncements need to be made by the representative person in a special way. Pronouncing a couple husband and wife is obviously an expression of the church and the congregation, even though the minister represents the state, as well as the church, in the pronouncement. A pronouncement should sound like a declaration, the announcement of a great fact.

In services of worship there are often words which are God's words to us and are not to be confused with the leader's words. Greetings to begin worship, calls to worship, declarations of pardon or absolution, and benedictions are most often classified as pronouncements. The "I baptize you" is clearly a pronouncement, just as is "The body of Christ, given for you" or other words of distribution. The wording of each will determine the category. In his revision of the Sacrament of the Lord's Supper, John Wesley changed the benediction to a less direct pronouncement: "The peace of God, which passeth all understanding" was changed to "May the peace . . ." In the latter the minister would more often assume a prayerful stance and probably bow the head and close the eyes. In the earlier form the words are a clear pronouncement to the people, and the representative person could properly look directly at the people to whom the words are addressed. My prime concern here is that the speaker know whose words are being spoken.

Those who feel unworthy to make such pronouncements must reexamine their role as ministers of the keys to the Kingdom granted by both baptism and ordination (Matt. 16:19). Through ordination, the church is authorizing someone to speak God's words with force and clarity.

Wide differences of opinion exist about the Call to Worship as a pronouncement. A growing tendency in some services and among some ministers is to begin the service with a greeting from minister to people. This can be a simple "Good morning" to which the people reply with the same, or much more elaborate words about how happy the minister is to see all the bright faces. There may very well be person to person words before the service begins as the people gather. However, it is of central importance for the leader and the congregation to know that we are called to worship by God. "Call to Worship" is being replaced by "Greeting" in new orders because it seems wrong to have the call come after the people have gathered, a prelude has been played, and a processional hymn sung. "Greeting," therefore, may seem more fitting, but the leaders should use words which leave no doubt about God's initiative in worship. Of course, these words are spoken by a person, because this is the way God speaks to us most of the time. The leader both speaks and hears God's words, and in no sense does the leader try to "play God." The leader must think through all these matters and then speak, continually being alert to discover whether the pronouncement is spoken and heard properly. If it isn't being comprehended, then the leader should be willing to try many expressions until spoken words and message are heard as one.

UNISON WORDS

An effective gauge to measure the participation of the congregation would be to register the number of words said together. Of course there is the danger of unison words becoming meaningless gibberish, but the risk seems worth it. A minister during the earlier days of this century who used to include the Lord's Prayer only occasionally explained the omission by saying unison words can lose their meaning. This is true not only of unison words; this is a risk taken in all worship. The important matter, however, seems to be that unless the prayer is said it will not be prayed. The danger of meaningless-ness or idolatry is always present, and the nearer we reach corporate worship the greater the danger of distortion. Idols are dangerous because they look so very much like God. The way to avoid idolatrous worship is not to give up worship, but to be willing to face the risks worship demands.

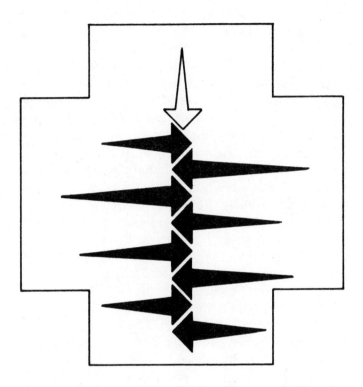

One unison word which affirms an idea is "amen." This word said by the people is a way for the congregation to join and make a prayer or other act of worship its own. Methodists have had the "amens" printed in boldface type for all their history, and until the present century the people spoke them out clearly. Today, many congregations have become more and more silent. This lack of participation has been covered up at times by having the choir sing responses, which only creates another barrier to acting together. The black church experience is having a profound influence on the worship of some Americans and is causing some of the silent to speak.

The most ordered unison speech in many congregations is that which is set to music. Hymns, songs, doxologies, responses, and other musical settings for any part of a service give worshipers the best opportunity for speaking together. This important fact points to the centrality of church music in worship and is about as near as this study will come to the field of church music. Psalms and the biblical canticles, which have furnished words of prayer and praise for Judeo-Christian worship, have very nearly been lost in those denominations where the singing of psalms has ceased.

There are encouraging signs of renewed interest in the psalms. Some ministers and music leaders are "lining out" psalms very much like they were sung in early American churches when books were rare and literacy was limited. The quality of praise is increased when a line of a psalm is sung to a free and simple tune by the leader and then repeated by the congregation. The simple tune is not a problem and the words which the people repeat carry the meaning. The responsive reading of psalms that are not well known often calls for concentration on words and pronunciations which distracts speakers so that they do not hear what they are saying. We must not deprive those who follow us of the resources in the book of Psalms. Psalms is so essential that every effort should be made to bring it back into our experience. All those concerned with the worship of the church must search for acceptable ways to make psalms available to the people. (See Resources at the end of this chapter.)

Spoken Words

There are unison words which the congregation already knows so the other necessary ingredient is leadership. The Lord's Prayer, affirmations of faith, litanies, and prayers in rituals for the Eucharist are known by the average worshiper. However, the leader needs to set the pace and keep it going. Leading unison readings does not call for domination by the leader, but it does require audible reading at a pace that is acceptable to the average person. There must not be the kind of individual interpretation that adds unexpected emphases and pauses. The minister who leads the congregation might well practice with the choir to come to some understanding of pace. A unison reading which is led too fast or too slow is a distraction from the intended purpose of the reading. There is no liturgical metronome to give the right speed, but a choir and minister practicing together can find the right pace for a congregation.

Increasing numbers of churches are preparing printed services so that the worshiper has the words in hand. The people are asked to read prayers, responses, and affirmations which they have never seen before and, in many cases, will never see again. This handbook will not deal with the preparation of such unison words in detail, but here are some matters to be kept in mind:

1. Unison words are personal but corporate. How does a congregation confess its sin and avoid individualistic sins?

2. Unison words are words in common use that are easily understood. Unison words express ideas quickly appropriated by readers.

3. The language is inclusive. There ought not to be any words which deliberately exclude anyone. This book is being written in a time when generic male pronouns are no longer acceptable, yet no new generic terms have been found. All unison words must be selected with care in order that a more inclusive language will evolve.

4. Printed unison words should be divided into phrases in such a way as to make their meanings obvious. Most new services are printed in sense lines to make reading and phrasing easier.

In the service I conducted discussed in the previous chapter, the congregation was asked in the Call to Confession to read over the prayer in silence. After an adequate pause, those who could make the prayer their own were invited to pray aloud together. There was enough favorable comment to make the practice the usual one in that service.

The experience of saying words of our faith with others is an affirmation of our membership in the Body of Christ. When death comes to a loved one and the church gathers for worship at the funeral service, the words of faith expressed in the Apostles' Creed can strengthen troubled and grieving persons as they say the "right" words at a time when words don't spring naturally to mind. And the hearing of those words all around one is to hear a living act of faith. In any given worship service how many of us face some specific situation to which the corporate expression of prayer or praise or affirmation brings new life?

READ WORDS

Charles Laughton often appeared in reading recitals in which he read from the Bible. Discussing these recitals in a television interview, he was asked why he had the Bible before him when he probably knew the passage by heart. He was quick to say that he knew the material backward and forward but that this was clearly a *reading*, and it should be presented as such. The Bible, which contains the record of the Word of God, ought to be *read* as a central act of worship. As worship leaders, ministers ought to work on their reading of the Scriptures with as much concern as they give to preaching and praying. A singer would never think of not practicing a solo, no matter how well known. For the same reasons, the one who reads the Scriptures in a service ought to practice, no matter how familiar the passage is.

Let us assume there is a fundamental awareness of speech concerns, such as volume, pitch, speed, and projection. There are good books on speech and each minister should have a framework for constant practice of excellent speech habits. Cassette tape recorders are inexpensive and accurate enough so that each leader of worship can practice with one. If the day should come when videotape is as easily available, this added dimension will be even more helpful for self-training and practice. Of course, self-help should be augmented by help from others. Without outside help from time to time we may only practice our mistakes.

After speech concerns are taken into account,

there is another concern in scripture reading which is essential for worship. The Word in the Bible must be given an opportunity to be expressed in the midst of the people. The reader is called to be one who is fully familiar with the passage and has comprehended the Word in it. A deep desire to have a passage heard as clearly as possible by the people listening will motivate the reader to be heard and understood. It is not a word from reader to people, it is a message to which the reader and the hearers listen.

Those who are accustomed to reading only a few verses from the Bible as a prelude to preaching often question the amount of time people will listen to Scripture lessons. Attention span depends not as much on time as it does on how the lessons are read. At least two generations of Christians have grown up in America who can be considered educated and yet are not familiar with the Bible. There are many reasons for such ignorance, but it has come about in part because the church has used the Bible less and less in worship services. Each passage read should contain a complete idea, which may require an adjustment in the lectionary assignments. Often a brief introduction by the reader will help the people comprehend more fully. In any case, the reading in itself is an important act of worship and if it is considered so by the reader and done so as to transmit this sense of importance, it will be listened to. Seldom have there been cases of mutiny over the amount of time subtracted from sermons and added to scriptures in order to read them well.

There is no consensus as to whether the reader

should maintain eye contact with the hearers. The issue is secondary to whether the passage is well comprehended, so it may be left to each reader to determine his or her own practice. Eye contact often varies with the situation. When Scripture is being read at a funeral, the biblical words may become the minister's words and eye contact may be quite proper. However the scripture is read, there should never be any doubt about the source of the words.

Laughton's name may have suggested "dramatic reading" as a model for liturgical reading, but this is not intended. There is also a school of thought that trains readers to read in a sort of chant that is supposed to present the passage as impersonally as possible, so that the listener is free to interpret. However, we cannot escape the fact that all reading is interpretation for good or ill. The reader runs the same risk with Scripture lessons that is confronted in all worship leadership, and that is the risk of manipulation while leading others. There is a purpose in the Scripture lesson that the church wants to communicate. The reader is a representative person in this office, and the risk of making a mistake must be recognized and taken.

Scripture lessons are often read by members of the congregation. Even so, the leader in charge of the service is still the person responsible for the effectiveness of the readings. Those who read should be selected well in advance and given the opportunity to practice in the church under guidance. All the concerns of good reading should be emphasized and checked. The passage and its meaning should be discussed. The values of wide congregational participation which are gained when different members read from the Bible during the service are not enough to make up for a lesson forfeited because it was read poorly. I still remember the power of a portion of the worship service in an English town many years ago when a layman read the lessons with clarity. That day the Word was read!

The church's liturgical literature also must be read. The sing-song of an oft-repeated phrase can be so distracting that its message doesn't get through. The same directions for reading the Bible apply to reading the rituals of the church.

A matter worth discussing in our churches is whether persons appropriate the message better when they are looking at the words being read or when the presentation is only heard. The presence of Bibles in pew racks is increasing and more and more leaders are giving page numbers so that the passage may be found readily. It may be that a well-read passage is clearer when the words are not seen by the hearers. Hearing and reading may compete or reinforce each other. Church rituals have usually included all the words of the service whether read in unison or not. Some rituals are now put in the hands of the congregation with careful use of ellipses (. . .) to indicate the omission of words and the place where responses are to follow. For instance, the Thanksgiving in *The Sacrament of the Lord's Supper, An Alternate Text, 1972* may be written in a bulletin in the following way:

It is right to give him thanks and praise.
Father, it is right that we should . . .

. . . and all your people now on earth
in worshiping and glorifying you:
Holy, holy, holy Lord, God of power and might.

Such a procedure saves space and may encourage
better understanding and participation in rituals if
the reading by the leader is done well.

PRAYERS

Prayer and worship are words which can be used
interchangeably, which is a good example of how
important the church believes prayer to be. Those
of us who are in a Free Church tradition frequently
reaffirm the danger of being locked into written
prayers, and yet a study of our orders of worship
shows how little praying there is in some of our
services. Some churches are deprived of the great
tradition of the literature of prayer and are not
given enough opportunities to pray. On the other
side of the coin, other congregations are exposed
only to the great prayers of the church and then are
not adaptable to freer expressions. Those who
prepare services of worship should realize that
there is a prayerful expression about every attitude
and emphasis of worship. Services, therefore,
might be arranged to give the people opportunities
to pray more often in much more specific areas of
concern.

The leader of worship must be alert to exactly

what a moment in the service demands and pray the prayer which best fits. Note the use of the words *pray* the prayer. This is a way of saying that the professional and representative pray-er for the church must be a person of faith who prays. The dearth in our life of prayer sometimes drives us to say empty words with great fervor. A ministerial tune can develop more quickly in prayer than any other area of our speech. In order to sound prayerful we add a bit more force to some words in order that conviction might be felt and heard. I don't know who started trying to hold the "d" in God, but I have heard three generations try it and fail. An impressive quiver is set up by the tremolo ministers affect in an effort to make "God" sound more like prayer than profanity—thus ministerial tunes develop. The handy cassette ought to be used inconspicuously in services so that the leader can correct any false sounds that may be there. There are authentic sounds of pleading, confession, thanksgiving, intercession, or any other attitude which each worship leader must find and express individually, but the inauthentic ones must go!

The vast literature of the church's *Common Prayer* ought to become a means of prayer for the church today. The leader of worship can use this literature as is or at least let it inform the prayers prepared for the congregation. We who are heirs of *The Book of Common Prayer*, directly or indirectly, have a literature of English language prayer of which we are stewards.[2] In addition to this heritage we are alive at a time when the greatness of this form of prayer is being replaced with a contemporary idiom. The Roman Catholics are moving from

Latin to English without the language of Thomas Cranmer and this is influencing all other churches.

In these transitional times some of us think in one idiom and must learn to speak in another. Those of us who were raised in a thee-and-thou tradition often find ourselves speaking in one era at the first of an extempore sentence and in another era at the end. This is a minor but valid reason for the leader to prepare prayers before the service whether they are actually read word for word or not. This does not in any way eliminate the usability of an inspiration at moments where advance preparation was not possible.

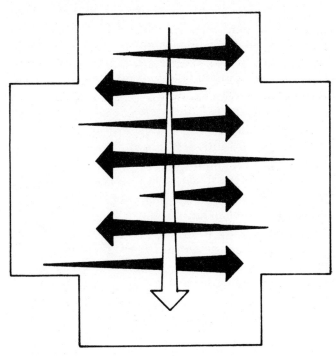

A practice of prayer which is becoming more widespread is the prayer of the people which gives individuals in the congregation an opportunity to make prayer requests or actually say a prayer to which the people will respond. It takes skill on the leader's part to make the people feel free to speak and also to include the whole community when individual concerns are expressed. The minister may need to put the concern into prayer form and then ask the congregation to respond with "Amen" or "This is our prayer" or "Lord, graciously hear" or another simple but genuine response. This form of congregational prayer is easier to lead in a community small enough to hear each other, yet a skillful leader can lead this form of prayer even in a very large congregation. When the minister paraphrases the concern expressed, the whole congregation has a opportunity to make the prayer its own more fully, thereby building a community of prayer on a deeper level. There are risks involved in spontaneity that threaten the "well-ordered" service. But readers should be encouraged to run those risks in order to help the whole community to pray.

One of the most important though maligned forms of prayer is the pastoral prayer. It has been called the wastebasket prayer or Magellan prayer (circumnavigating the globe) and where it is not criticized it is squirmed through. But there is an important place for the pastor as a concerned representative person to pray for and on behalf of the people. The pastoral prayer ought to be specific enough to be the prayer of a specific congregation, general enough to be suitable for corporate worship, timely enough in the light of the Eternal, and concise enough to be brief but not sound superficial. In praying the pastoral prayer, the pastor's office is manifest in one of the most important priestly services to God and to the church.

SERMONS

In some sections of America the most common title for ministers is preacher. The appellation may be more prayer than title because the members of the church are still asking their minister to preach. The worship service is not just a preaching time; it is the church in common worship. We need to get this important message across by making the entire worship vital—including the sermon. A host of good homiletics textbooks are in print and every minister should have mastered at least one of them. There is also a spate of books about preaching and preachers which come out from time to time and act like new invitations to preach with hope and confidence. (See Resources section for this chapter.) This book leaves to these other guides their important purpose. A handbook on worship leadership ought to say as clearly as possible that there is no value in discussing which role in a worship service is most important. If anything ought to be done when the church gathers for worship it ought to be done well as an offering to God.

What is the sermon? It is of the essence of the church, a part of worship where the "pure word of God is preached." Ernest Best speaks of the biblical record as a collection of crystallizations of the meaning of the gospel and of sermons as new crystallizations or precipitations.[3] Robert W. Hovda speaks of preaching as clowning and asks preachers "to be fools, jesters, given to fancy, who don't mind dressing up . . . and doing unproductive things. The clown function in a social group is related to the critical function and also to the relieving function of one who helps everybody escape from social pressure for a moment."[4]

The image of the preacher as clown is not a call to be false, but to be as honest as a clown may be able to be. Frederick Buechner would probably agree with Hovda, but he adds another dimension when he calls preachers to be honestly themselves and tell the truth as it is experienced by the preacher. He says the "task of the preacher is to hold up life to us; by whatever gifts he or she has of imagination, eloquence, simple candor, to create images of life through which we can somehow see into the wordless truth of our lives. Before the Gospel is good news, it is simply the news that that's the way it is, whatever day it is of whatever year."[5]

The sermon is like a flower. It has its roots in the biblical faith expressed in a passage (often found in the lectionary); it grows in the traditions of the faith and blossoms in the midst of the time and place where the hearing congregation lives its life. It may be a written word, but it certainly is not a read word. Even if it is written on paper in front of the preacher, it must be a lively word between speaker and hearers. The sermon is a message of life that has brought the speaker to life; the preacher in turn offers this flower to all who will accept life. The sermon is a brand new version of an old, old story we ask to hear over and over again. The message doesn't need to be great, just true and clear and alive. The sermon really is THE announcement for the day. The sermon is the story of the congregation, an offering from the preacher that can also become the offering of the people. The words can become God's Word—but that is God's miracle as only God can will it.

Resources

To help in restoring Psalms as a vital means of worship, the following books are suggested:

Gelineau, Joseph. *The Psalms: Singing Version*. New York: Paulist Press, 1968. See also the Gelineau musical settings.

Lutheran Book of Worship. Minneapolis: Augsburg Publishing House, 1979.

Routley, Erik. *Music Leadership in the Church*. Nashville: Abingdon, 1967. Chapters 5 and 6.

Shepherd, Massey H. *The Psalms in Christian Worship, A Practical Guide*. Minneapolis: Augsburg Publishing House, 1976.

———. ed. *A Liturgical Psalter for the Christian Year*. Minneapolis: Augsburg Publishing House; Collegeville: The Liturgical Press.

Story, Quinn, and Wright, eds. *Morning Praise and Evensong*. Notre Dame, Ind.: Fides Publishers, 1973.

Some good textbooks on preaching are:

Davis, H. Grady. *Design for Preaching*. Philadelphia: Fortress Press, 1958. A personal preference whose many editions indicate its value.

Hoefler, Richard Carl. *Creative Preaching and Oral Writing.* Lima, Oh.: C.S.S. Publishing Company, 1978. We are going to give this a trial in seminary classes partly because students don't find Davis as helpful as I wish they did.

Jones, Ilion T. *Principles and Practice of Preaching.* Nashville: Abingdon, 1956.

Some books that help keep you preaching:

Classics:

Barth, Karl. *The Preaching of the Gospel.* Philadelphia: Westminster Press, 1963.

Coffin, Henry Sloane. *Communion Through Preaching.* New York: Scribner's, 1952.

Knox, John. *The Integrity of Preaching.* Nashville: Abingdon, 1957.

Current:

Buechner, Frederick. *Telling the Truth: The Gospel as Tragedy, Comedy and Fairy Tale.* New York: Harper & Row, 1977.

Keck, Leander E. *The Bible in the Pulpit.* Nashville: Abingdon, 1978.

THREE

Visible Words

In the early days of radio in America, station WBT in Charlotte, North Carolina, invited Tryon Street Methodist Church to broadcast its services. The stewards discussed the matter at some length and declined the invitation because it might keep people at home listening to the broadcasts instead of attending the services. First Baptist Church accepted the invitation and people flocked to see Dr. Luther Little, whom they were hearing on the radio. Church attendance increased sharply because people want to see as well as hear. For twenty years outstanding preachers across the United States were heard by hosts of listeners on the radio, and because of these broadcasts their church attendance grew dramatically.

FACIAL EXPRESSIONS

The reason people wanted to see the person behind the radio voice in pre-TV days was to find out what he looked like. Some of the better-known announcers drew large crowds when they traveled about on speaking engagements. The news segments between the feature motion pictures were watched with great interest because people could *see* what they had heard about. The verdict on the influence of television on political office is not yet in, but that it is of great importance is unquestioned.

The influence of Harry Emerson Fosdick and his contemporaries in the early days of radio was a boon to local churches. However, the impact of television evangelism has often become a financial bonanza for the evangelist and has not strengthened local congregations. Televising local worship services is a service to church members who are unable to attend. A discussion of the implications of these ideas would take us on tangents far removed from the facial expression of the minister. Keep in mind, though, that we are being seen by people who customarily watch on TV persons who know the importance of facial expressions and have learned skills in their use.

The leader of worship must take into account facial expressions as a part of leadership effectiveness. I feel a certain hesitation in bringing up the matter for fear I may suggest to some that ministers need a "worship face." This would fall into the category of ministerial tunes—good intentions gone awry. Working on a facial expression to communicate certain attitudes can be done best by thinking about the meaning of the words (expressed or unexpressed) and openly showing how one feels. A face trying to look faithful may look more like a cry for relief from indigestion than like an expression of faith. How should we look when we say we join Paul in his conviction that neither death nor life can separate us from the love of God? Tie facial expressions to these words, then determine how words and face could communicate. A smile trying to show "joy in the Lord" may spill over into related ideas that call for no smile—then we become living illustrations of the Cheshire Cat.

It would be wrong to assume, however, that ideas expressed with the right words will automatically result in a good facial expression. To say with our lips and express with our faces the same idea is something we must learn. In personal conversations there is enough feedback so that we know when we are understood. There is much less feedback in a congregation, but there are ways an alert pastor can know what is communicated. Videotape is a great device for teaching homiletics, and it can also be helpful to see one's style as a leader of a worship service. The facial expressions of the speaker are so important that help should be sought from any who are able to be constructive critics. The TV camera can pan to the face of the speaker and show the most subtle facial expression. A minister, standing several feet from the nearest person, cannot rely on facial expressions suitable in close conversation because they simply do not span the greater distance. The furrowed brow in a close conversation doesn't furrow enough at thirty feet. And although the sweeping gesture and affected grimace may be acceptable in some pantomime, they are not appropriate in the pulpit. The leader of worship needs to practice being *seen* and ask for help in matching sight and distance with sound.

GESTURES AND POSTURES

The face, of course, is a part of the body and it may be the most expressive part of the body in accompanying speech, but the whole body "speaks." Present studies of body language put a great deal of meaning in movements, even to the point of implying that our motions don't lie; yet actions can be misunderstood as well as spoken words. The overall effect of body and speech, however, does add up to a message. There are some persons who, when they speak, are virtually immobile, and if a message is communicated, there is certainly no need to impose actions artificially. Conversely, there are those whose motions are so overdone that they become distractions.

As a way of finding the best relationship between words and actions, watch yourself when telling a story to a child. It may be that those leaders of worship who seem like pillars of salt, on the one hand, or windmills, on the other, should face the demands of making the story of Goldilocks come to life for a three-year-old. This is a more exacting demand than a church service, but if it can be done well, the church will profit by the learning. Children will listen if they can participate through all their senses, and their participation will be no better than the full participation of the storyteller. Full participation may require acting the part of the various bears or eating bowls of porridge of different temperatures. The child demands a wide variety of verbal emphases, facial expressions, and body motions. It may not be necessary to break down a baby bed, but one's motions should be concrete enough to be understood.

Those of us in denominations who do not often make the sign of the cross lack a ritual act of reverence which is needed. Vatican II eliminated most of the signs of the cross from the Mass because overuse detracted from the meaning. Those who have no comparable gesture need to discover its value. The motion of the hand in the shape of a cross in benedictions, blessings, and pronouncements of all kinds seems quite fitting in many circumstances.

The leader of worship must always be aware that the motions and postures of leadership are both symbolic and real. Standing for praise or bowing for prayer both require full physical expression. Some motions have become so reserved as to lose their meaning. A good example of this is the gentle touching of the chest in the penitential rite of the Roman Mass when confessing our own faults. The rubric says "all strike their breast," yet the act is usually far from striking. However, even a grievous fault could be overstated by beating the breast in contrition.

Generations ago, the rubric about meeting the body at the gate of the church and processing to the chancel was fitting for the village church during a funeral in Europe or America. The minister entering a funeral home chapel today faces real difficulty in knowing what actions to use in symbolizing a supporting community of faith. Inside a church, the minister, leading the procession of the coffin, the pallbearers, and the family, enacts an important message of the faith of the church at the time of death. The presence of the minister at the coffin saying the name of the deceased at the beginning of the service and at the committal is an act which gives needed particularity.

A funeral is largely an enactment of faith. In pioneer America the funeral service was very much closer to the need for building a box, digging a grave, lowering the coffin, and replacing the earth. Some ministers today will still remember that the first act after the benediction was filling the grave back up. Artificial grass and motorized lowering devices are relatively recent additions to funerals. There is the need to deal with the realities of death and grief, but the actual motions of the disposal of a dead body are best handled by well-trained and equipped funeral directors. Today the funeral service includes more symbolic acts of burial than actual. Some services emphasize lowering the coffin and throwing dirt into the grave, but these services only indicate that actions express more fully what words only symbolize. Any practice that tries to avoid the reality of death is wrong; however, realism does not necessarily mean a public display of all aspects of death. Plastic grass may indeed be a help in covering the work of a backhoe and flowers more suitable than a large hole in the ground, but funeral ceremonies should free people to express grief and support and love and faith.

The motions of a wedding have undergone many changes, and the present ferment of ideas will probably institute changes not even imagined now. According to present-day trends, the congregation gathers in as unobtrusive a way as possible. This may be a symbol of viewing marriage as a decision between two persons (the bride and groom only) rather than a decision involving two extended families, at least one congregation, and society at large. I have no particular suggestions here for new ceremonials, but there is a need for new ones. The wedding procession visualized in all our etiquette books is based on the assumption that the bride is given away by her father. This is not an acceptable view of the place of the bride in marriage today and should be changed. Some wedding services incorporate acts and responses by each family as they release one member and accept another, thereby creating a whole new relationship all around. Ministers must be alert to find both words and ceremonials which will communicate the message of Christian marriage as clearly as possible.

In planning for any public service there is a need for choreography. The relationships of meanings in words, postures, movements, facial expressions, and sounds must be coordinated carefully. Often this coordination is natural and "right." Sometimes what seems quite natural to the leader is awkward to observers. For instance, a bride and groom may naturally look at the minister as he gives them the words to say to each other in their pledge of faith. In this case, however, it is not good to look at the person speaking, but to the person spoken to. At this time in a wedding the bride and groom should face and speak to each other—the minister is only the prompter.

At a service of renewal of baptism a minister was taking water in her hand and sprinkling it toward the people as she said, "Remember your baptism and be thankful." A person standing next to the aisle saw this gesture as an antagonistic one and said in a stage whisper, "I could spit on you!" At least to one person in the congregation the hand was turning the words into a lie. This is another illustration of the need for feedback from the pew if leaders are to learn.

In worship, the leader must see to it that the acts enhance the meanings of the service and avoid awkward motions that are unrelated or actually detract from the purposes of the service.

The act of standing for praise is virtually universal. The orientation during praise varies. In recent years Methodists often turned and faced the cross on the chancel wall or the altar table at the singing of a doxology or the saying of a creed. Now that the altar table is moved forward in many of the churches that once had the table against the wall, it is probably more fitting to make the altar table the point toward which people face. In any case, a posture that reinforces the community worshiping together before God is desirable.

Churches are learning all kinds of ways in which to act in prayers. Directions given in most pre-1970 service books are confined to kneeling or bowing for prayer. The rubrics in the Methodist *Book of Worship* (1964) for the conduct of the Sacrament of the Lord's Supper direct that the minister should kneel "facing the Lord's Table" at the Prayer of General Confession, the Prayer of Consecration, Prayer of Humble Access, and again at the closing Prayer of Thanksgiving. In the years since that service was published, most of Christendom has brought the Lord's Table forward and the minister stands behind it in what is called the basilican position. This is much more suitable in enacting the church gathered around the table for the common meal. In a forward-facing, standing position the minister can be clearly heard, and with the hands and head can show an attitude of prayer that communicates the nature of the particular prayer.

In buildings where the altar is fixed to the back of the chancel wall, portable altar tables are frequently used at the front of the chancel. If the portable table is covered with a cloth it blends inconspicuously with the rest of the chancel furniture. In this way the service can be conducted with the people gathered around the table instead of before the altar. This does not eliminate the message of sacrifice where the offering is transformed into newness of life, but the central Christian experience represented by eating and drinking *around* a table becomes more obvious.

For a prayer of confession the kneeling or bowing on the part of the leader as well as the rest of the congregation seems fitting as a symbol of humility, vulnerability, and dependence. If it is possible for the leader to kneel and speak so as to be heard, all the better. If the minister goes out of both sight and sound he or she is not helpful as a leader. Words of grace and pardon ought, of course, to be said from a standing position to the people, who are either standing or sitting upright.

Standing for prayer is an ancient posture which fell into disuse when our services became dominated by an almost unrelieved penitential mood. Today we are getting to our feet. "And he said to me,

'Son of man, stand upon your feet, and I will speak to you.' And when he spoke to me, the Spirit entered into me and set me upon my feet; and I heard him speaking to me" (Ezek. 2:1-2 RSV). Ezekiel was faithful to the practice of his people in standing up for prayer—both for praying to God and listening to God's words. Prayers of invocation, praise and thanksgiving, petition and intercession, may well be done when standing or when the people are alert and thoughtful while sitting. Where congregations unite in prayers which are spoken by individuals and shared with the whole community, responses can be made with heads up and eyes open. Enlarging the scope of the prayers of the church may be encouraged by learning many postures of prayer to reflect their deeper dimensions.

The gestures and postures of the leader must be done smoothly and relate as closely as possible to every word and attitude. Some movements will come quite naturally and others will need to be learned, and we must recognize that any new learning feels awkward for a time. A benediction pronounced while looking at a congregation with arms extended to the side and palms open may not seem natural at first, but it does express the intention of the moment very well. Placing my hands on the heads of the kneeling bride and groom to pronounce the blessing seems proper now, but it didn't "feel right" at first.

No action can be considered insignificant, and the leader and planning team ought to consider all actions for their naturalness and suitability. The way in which bread is given and received in Holy Communion gives meaning to the whole transaction. The way the hands are used in baptism, confirmation, and ordination carry messages of theological significance. There is no limit to the concern for worship as an *act* of the people.

USES OF SPACE

The language of the actions of the worship leader must be seen in relation to where the actions take place. There are no specific rules about the uses of space for worship, but our worship should be using more of the space provided. Too often we cluster at a liturgical center rather than use the whole room to suggest the many aspects of the Christian message. If the whole room is used as space for worship, there ought to be clear designations for different activities. The location of the minister when presiding, reading, preaching, praying, conducting the sacraments, can serve to reinforce the meaning of each act. In some of our traditions where preaching is central, the pulpit is the spot from which the whole service is conducted. Churches built in recent years have made chancels more spacious, but the location of microphones has often been a dominant factor in tying the minister to a few places or demanding skill in avoiding cords. There must be ways out of this electronic bondage. Voice projection and good acoustics may be a place to start.

There is no value in a minister's hopping about just to keep the people guessing, but there is value in having different places from which the leader leads the people: for instance, announcements may be made from the front of the center aisle; prayers of the people may be spoken in the pews with the minister standing in the aisle near the speaker. The liberation of the minister from any "locked in" position can free the whole congregation to use all the space in the room to augment the message. Some churches are being built with flexible seating which allows room arrangements to match particular worship services. Sturdy, comfortable chairs made for this purpose are now available. With a movable seating arrangement, the use of the worship room becomes more versatile and the means of congregational worship more dynamic.

FOUR

The Use of Things

USES OF THINGS

Protestants have had a difficult time with a doctrine of creation which helps us clarify our attitude toward things. The Reformation raised the question about sacred objects. The iconoclasts, who went about destroying statues and images, took the reformers with great seriousness and tried to destroy what they believed was an erroneous message. We can be grateful that the white heat of their fear, anger, and disagreement has subsided. It would be tragic, however, if the ashes represented unconcern. Christians of all denominations must come to a deeper understanding about *things* as a means of grace. There is a sense in which Roman Catholics accept the sacredness of some things in themselves. Pilgrimages to Lourdes or Fatima or the light burning at the altar where the Host is reserved indicate a reverence for a particular place or thing. A sign saying that visitors should not enter the chancel of Duke University Chapel may say the same thing, even though there may be little theological discussion underlying the sign. Many a Protestant home has a table on which sits a Bible, and nothing is ever laid on top of it. No highway is built until every effort has been made to move a grave that would be in the right-of-way. As you read this page, look around and spot those things in your home or study which you reverence whether you call them holy or not.

While we are still looking for adequate doctrines about things, it is important for us to affirm the seriousness of the use of things. A worship leader is called to use many things, and the way in which they are used will communicate the truths that certain things represent.

Protestants are committed to the foundational place of the biblical record. In most churches the Bible as book is an important symbol. But the Bible as symbol must be used. Some churches have a beautiful copy of the Bible displayed in a prominent place from which no one ever reads! Such "use" of the Bible is a negative symbol. The sign or symbol of the unread Bible may be a mark of our sickness that pays only lip service to reading and hearing the Word. On the other hand, the Bible often sits on the altar table, where it becomes buried in a confusion of symbols. The Bible ought to be placed where it can be both seen as a symbol and read from to the people gathered. The old three-decker pulpit seen in eighteenth-century English churches gave a very vivid message about the place of the Bible and preaching. Wesley Chapel, recently restored in London, has a place for Bible reading and preaching, which clearly communicates its importance to the whole congregation. From the late 1920s until about 1960, Methodist churches frequently divided the chancel, with the lectern on one side and the pulpit on the other. That traditional use of the chancel designated the north side as the Gospel side and the south side as the Epistle side made no difference, however, in Methodist practice. (Architecturally, north is to the left as one faces the chancel.) The shape of Methodist churches has often reflected sociological and economic forces more than ecclesiastical or theological ones.

The liturgical focus on the Bible should point quite sharply to the reading, hearing, and expounding of the Word. A lectern that swivels so that the Bible can be seen by the congregation as well as turned and read to the people fulfills two important functions.

The leader of worship should use the Bible in such a way as to add an important message to good reading. Roman Catholic services have a ceremonial that emphasizes the importance of the Word. The use of candles, processionals with the Book, incense, responses, all say "hear this" in a dramatic way. The standing for the reading of a selection from the first four books of the New Testament seems to me to be a fundamental misunderstanding of the nature of the Gospel. If standing is the best way to hear the Gospel, then the congregation should stand for each reading. Thoughtful and reverent comprehension of the reading from the Bible may best be done while seated and alert. This is a matter each congregation might do well to study and discuss. No matter what ceremonial is used, the act in itself ought to say what the church believes about the Bible and the reading of it.

Offering plates are things which sometimes sit empty on the altar table. When filled, they frequently are removed to the "counting house," and the offering is not brought to the table. A plate filled with symbols of our lives (money) should be brought to the place of sacrifice and presented in the faith that these gifts can be transformed into new life. The use of the plate and the table becomes the means of an action which God can make sacred. One can say the same for any thing in the church—unlit candles cry out on behalf of darkness; unused things that ought to be used send undesirable messages.

Baptism and Eucharist are actions with things. The words of the sacraments are related to acts inseparably, and the minister is ordained to say and to do. Flamboyant overaction can damage a service, but hiding action is the more frequent abuse. The element used in baptism is water. Churches which use the method of sprinkling have tended to make the water nearly invisible. Bonbon-dish fonts brought for the occasion to the altar table are hardly adequate to show washing, cleansing, or outpouring. The symbolizing of death and resurrection is seriously strained with such tiny amounts of water.

The sacrament of baptism has many meanings and three historic modes. The act of initiation into the Body of Christ, the act of being given a Christian name, the act of participating in the death and resurrection of Jesus Christ, and other related meanings are not easily manifested by immersion, pouring, or sprinkling. Water is the central element in baptism and the baptized person as well as those who watch must know that water is the sacramental element. A few drops of water on the hand (often

69

flung off before their use) are of little value as signs or symbols. A pitcher or shell used to pour water on the head has been a useful vessel for centuries. Flowers are not usually mentioned, yet there are some who need to be reminded that rose buds and colored carnations detract from the baptismal element and should not be part of the ceremony. In baptism enough water should be used to let the symbol be seen, felt, and heard. For the minister, "enough" water means a towel will be needed to dry the hands after the ceremony, so a towel should be provided at the font.

The minister's taking the child into his or her arms as an act of receiving a new member is an important message. With children and adults, using enough water from the hand to run down forehead and neck is a visual symbol that adds meaning to the minister's words. The sign of the cross on the forehead can be an act that also symbolizes a new membership in the name of God: Father, Son, and Holy Spirit. Oil is used in many churches when the sign of the cross is made, but it is not yet customary among Methodists.

We need to remember that baptism is a symbolic cleansing, marking, and sharing in the death and resurrection of Jesus Christ. Those who immerse for baptism must avoid all aspects of the service that detract from the chief meanings of the sacrament. Churches which have built baptistries for immersions usually make it possible for the congregation to see candidates baptized, but move them quickly out of sight to dry and dress. Those baptized in rivers and pools often become more noticeable for being soaking wet than for being new members of the church.

As a United Methodist, I commend to our denomination a much more serious study of the meaning of baptism and a search for ways to have the ceremonial of baptism done in the midst of the congregation at worship. It is a scandal bordering on heresy that has allowed us to turn baptism into the dedication of a child by well-intentioned parents or sponsors. The sacrament of baptism is not a time for us to do God a favor but for us to celebrate the favor of God's initiating grace.

The Eucharist, the Sacrament of the Lord's Supper, is a doing, an acting with things. Gregory Dix in his *Shape of the Liturgy*[1] has reminded all Christians of the fourfold action of the Eucharist: taking bread and cup, giving thanks, breaking bread, giving bread and cup. The words define the meanings, and the actions enlighten and embody this ancient and current expression of the Gospel. The primary meanings of Holy Communion must be a subject of constant study, however. The way in which the sacrament is conducted can be another point where important secondary considerations become means of receiving and comprehending God's grace. Experiencing God's presence in the worship of the congregation is more to be appropriated than analyzed, yet study can amplify and improve the experience.

The elements of the Eucharist are bread and wine used in a common meal by the congregation as it eats and drinks together and participates in the reality of Jesus Christ. There are a number of other ways in which we gather in the Lord's name and know his presence, but the Lord's Supper is the service by which the church has most often celebrated its faith. Holy Communion also testifies to the divisions among Christians and stands as the one service in which we cannot now unite.

We will be concerned, therefore, that the service be conducted in a way in which most members of a congregation can unite. The basic element fundamental to the service is the gathered congregation. Anything which can be done to help the congregation know that it is a community of persons united should be tried. Most churches that are using new services of worship have regained what the Eastern churches never lost—the Peace. Affirming one another, through words and acts, as a community of forgiven and reconciled people threatens those who had come to expect being left alone in worship, but it has opened up new opportunities for expressing our relationship with others in God's name. Honoring the integrity of persons must be done in all worship, but confronting us more urgently is how we can honor our membership with one another in the Body of Christ. The Passing of the Peace is symbolic and probably is not a time for reconciling profound differences between persons before eating together, yet should be more than just a nod from side to side.

Here is another personal word about a helpful experience that I have had in leading worship: The minister in the narthex *before* the service adds a whole new dimension to the leader's attitude toward the congregation, and there is reason to believe such an activity makes some difference with members of the congregation. People bring

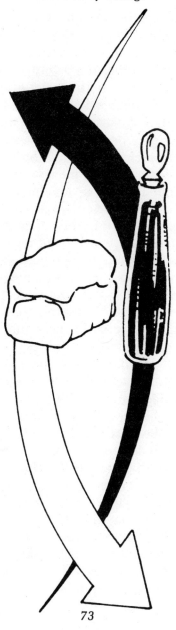

many joys and sorrows and doubts and routines and surprises to church. We are called to preach in the midst of the people, and this time before the service can be another opportunity for forming a deeper relationship to the congregation. If the minister needs those last few minutes to get a word from the Lord, it may be a bit late in the vestry and the Lord just may be speaking in the vestibule!

The central elements of the Lord's Supper are bread and wine. (In many places wine is not used and unfermented juice is the element. As in the Bible, this book will refer to wine and hope that each congregation will find its element sacramental.) A parenthetical word is not necessary in the same way about bread, though there are many who insist on wine who use quite inadequate substitutes for bread. The planning team for worship needs to work diligently on the conduct of Holy Communion. A concern for the confidence of the people along with the faithfulness to the gospel must be kept in mind at all times. A number of issues are at hand, and there are few places where only one answer is clear.

What service is to be used? How often?

How can it be conducted to emphasize thanksgiving to God above all else? How can the worshiper feel involved in the Holy Communion throughout the service?

How can the congregation feel that the bread and wine are brought as gifts from the people? An actual bringing of the elements from the entrance is often done effectively. A particular family might bring bread or wine which they have made.

How can the bread be broken and served to the

people? Communion wafers are not like any other bread we eat. Some bits of bread sold for communion are so small as to be difficult to pick up. The direction to place bread into the hand of the communicant is difficult to fulfill when these small crumbs are used. Should we use unleavened bread, matzo? Should we use a loaf that can be broken?

How should the congregation drink together? Should the common cup be offered by a minister or designated server? Should individual cups be used? Is it possible to dip the bread into a common cup (called intinction)?

Should the people be served while kneeling at the chancel rail? Should they stand together in the chancel? The Reformed practice of laypersons serving the people in the pews is a choice of many. Should that be done in this congregation?

Does the time it takes to serve this congregation matter?

What vessels and linens should be used? How are they cared for?

Different "right" answers can be given to each of the questions above or any others that should concern the congregation. It is quite clear from the United Methodist *Alternate Service 1972* that there is strong advocacy for the use of a loaf of bread. This service is highly commended for its rubrics and words found in "The Breaking of the Bread and the Taking of the Cup." This should be a whole act in itself in full view of the people. In Holy Communion the eating and drinking are symbolic of a whole meal as well as symbols of the life given us by Jesus Christ. A broken piece of bread placed in my hand can and does symbolize that which I am given—food indispensable for life itself. This act carries more of the message of the Eucharist than taking bread and cup at a self-service altar rail. Pew distribution, with its history among Reformed churches, seems to express the Word more visibly than the self-service method, which has been practiced in many churches built since World War II.

Many large Methodist congregations have tried to serve the Lord's Supper without taking an unusually long time. Kneeling rails have been equipped with trays of bread and cups accessible to all who kneel at any place along the rail. A minister, often standing in the pulpit, will say the words of distribution. The worshiper will take the bread and the cup, and then those at the rail at that time are dismissed. Such a method diminishes the act of giving and receiving which is so central to the Sacrament. The dismissal of the "tables," no matter how the elements are distributed, tends to fragment the congregation. Receiving the elements while standing and moving past the servers is often done. Those who wish to kneel may do so after being served. A "continuous table" where the people leave after being served and others take their place and are served at once is a method which does not take so long. The unity of the whole congregation is maintained when the action flows with ease and the people are aware that the sacrament is not confined only to the act of receiving bread and wine. Singing hymns during the distribution also enhances the sense of unity of the congregation's worship.

Individual cups and awareness of germs are probably closely related. Millions of persons have known the sacramental presence of Christ as they drank together with their companions of the Way and received the fruit of the True Vine from individual cups—their means to Christ ought not to be scorned as they are in much current literature. But how might congregations take the wine and share it among themselves best? Intinction has been found satisfactory in many places recently. Robert Hovda does raise some disturbing questions when he says it is neither eating nor drinking.[2] If we keep Hovda's assertion in mind, intinction can be a viable method for those whose objections to drinking from the same cup are strong. In Robert W. Jenson's book, *Visible Words: The Interpretation and Practice of Christian Sacraments*, he leaves little room for anything but a cup of red wine with two handles which can be passed from one person to another.[3] This may be too fixed a pattern, but his plea for the service to show itself as a common meal among all the people gathered is an important point that cannot be made too strongly.

If hymns are sung by the congregation during the distribution of the elements at the chancel, the sense of participation in the service by all members will be increased. To give the impression that Holy Communion is confined to the few moments when the person receives the elements is a mistake. Silence can be a setting for the service that encourages a sense of community. Though organists and some others may object to "walking music," quiet instrumental music can establish a sense of "silence" during the reception of the bread and wine.

The motions of the minister as the elements are

handled are a message to those who see, and the congregation ought to see. The bread and cup are quite ordinary things from everyday life. The extraordinary reality of the presence of God is made known in just the use of these things. Fine silver chalices bejeweled with costly stones are offerings in themselves, but it is the staff of the food of life eaten and drunk by faithful people which is the bearer of God. The minister and all the members are called to receive this new epiphany with thanksgiving. How does one handle the bread and wine? Not immobilized by awe, certainly; yet being flippant and casual before such a miracle is insensitive. Let the elements themselves be central—neither our woe nor joy nor gratitude seems of primary importance. The breaking of the bread, the pouring of the wine, and their distribution with decisive acts among persons are the things that are important.

In the course of a worship service many things are used. The leader should be concerned that the use of things becomes as clear to the viewers as words are to the hearers. Lighting a candle, lifting a book, holding a plate, breaking a loaf, or handling any other thing should be an important dimension of meaning. When their use is an accepted ritual of the community, it ought to be deliberate enough to be clear and natural enough to be smoothly assimilated. Throwing dirt into a grave should be obvious to those in sight of the motion, and the handful of earth ought not to be picked up by the person as if there were a fear of being soiled. Every leader should think through and act out the use of things before a public performance.

VESTMENTS

Elbert Russell, a Quaker and dean of the seminary at Duke University (Methodist) from 1928 to 1941, is said to have been invited to preach at an Episcopal Church where he was asked if he would wear a robe. "Do I have to?" he asked. "Oh, no!" he was told. "I'll wear one, then," he replied. The story may be apocryphal, but Dean Russell could easily have said this; he trained a number of us to believe in such an attitude toward vestments. It was partly the influence of Duke Chapel, where robes were used from its opening in 1932, that robes came to be worn in the Methodist pulpits in that region. There were few Methodist ministers wearing vestments anywhere in the United States at that time. Hundreds of men who went into the chaplaincy of the armed forces began to wear robes and stoles for the first time during World War II, and they returned to spread the practice throughout the country.

Actually, robes were first introduced in the choirs of Methodist churches and many other denominations after World War I. There were great debates in the churches about robes for the choir, and many viewed this "Romish" practice with alarm. Most congregations accepted robes for the choir in order that this highly visible group be less individually conspicuous and that the unity of the choir be affirmed. The widespread use of choir robes did not prevent later debates over robes for the minister. The discussion about vestments is different in each denomination, and even within

79

the denominations. I am writing as one Methodist in a time when we can examine the uses of liturgical vestments for clergy without many precedents. We can rejoice in the freedom this unprecedented situation offers in the same way some Roman Catholic priests can now decide to wear street clothes in the celebration of the Eucharist.

Each congregation may well study its own situation and begin to discuss liturgical vestments for the worship in their church. There are not many books that speak to the immediate situation, but there are occasional articles on vestments appearing from time to time that will help. The Art Institute of Chicago prepared a catalogue for a vestment exhibit in 1975.[4] Of especial interest in this catalogue are essays on the Roman, Anglican, and Protestant situations in regard to vestments. A study of these essays can give a brief and helpful view of the current situation.

A review of Cokesbury catalogues, the retail division of The United Methodist Publishing House, will show that since 1945 there has been an increasing emphasis on pulpit gowns. This could be a reflection of the selling edge that lags a bit behind the growing edge. In 1960 the formal picture of the bishops of The Methodist Church had them garbed in black gowns and academic hoods. Two of them had on clerical collars, all had velvet panels on the robes, and some of the panels were red or purple—but most of them were black. In the most recent pictures the bishops are wearing stoles over the black robes. The colors of the panels and the doctoral stripes represent a variety of styles and tastes. In the 1979 Cokesbury catalogue robes were offered in several styles and colors, clerical shirts seem to have been dyed along with Easter eggs, and prices reflect inflation.

Alongside the "Wesley" robes offered by Cokesbury are albs. This garment is becoming a widely accepted vestment in several denominations. It is a simple garment with sleeves that are usually narrow and never as full as the academic or Geneva gowns. The alb is either white or off-white and may be worn with or without a cincture, or belt. It reaches the feet. In many Methodist congregations it is worn by the minister with a stole. The way in which the stole is worn around the neck or over a shoulder in Roman and Orthodox Churches designates order. In Methodist churches the stole is worn around the neck. The alb and stole have become widely accepted in congregations across America.

Methodists are accepting the stole as a symbol of ordination, and it is being worn more widely than any other liturgical garment. Some Annual Conferences are giving a stole at ordination. It is not necessary to have a rule in *The Book of Discipline* about the use of the stole to make it widely accepted as a sign of the ordained clergy. As a badge marking this representative person the stole can be a liturgical expression of the church at worship.

The use of stoles by choirs frequently adds a colorful decoration to the choir robe. This use of color can be achieved with a collar or neck-piece which improves the appearance of the choir without the questionable use of a stole. Churches and suppliers of choir vestments ought to talk with each other before the catalogues are published!

A few United Methodist ministers wear a chasuble at Holy Communion. This is a garment used in celebrating the Eucharist in the Roman Church that became one of the most elaborate. Today the Roman Church directs that the value of the vestment is in its material and form and warns against much ornamentation. Some of the chasubles made today are quite plain, circular overgarments with few if any symbols. The symbols on the back of the older chasubles were to be seen when the priests faced the altar. A chasuble used in a Methodist church by the minister in the Sacrament of the Lord's Supper raises the same "Romish" questions that were raised when robes for the choir or clergy were introduced.

If it ever becomes mandatory that United Methodists wear a uniform, we will have forgotten our understanding of worship. We ought to be free to ask the important questions and explore various answers, and many of us in a wide segment of Christendom are that free today.

What are liturgical garments for? If a particular person is to be in a representative role in worship, why should the clothing be different? If the vestments set the leader apart from the congregation, and that only, then vestments are a disservice. The alb was first worn at a time when most people wore such tunics. In the early twentieth century, professional men wore Prince Albert coats and later morning coats or cutaways. When fashions changed and people changed to other styles, the priests held on to the albs. When other professional men began to wear only sack coats, some ministers were still wearing morning coat, winged collar, and striped trousers to lead worship. One can see this sort of situation in some camp or resort retreats when the minister dresses for leading worship as if in the city. This may be a way of wearing our "Sunday best" as a kind of offering to God, though it does seem incongruous. When I was the pastor of a new congregation in Houston, Texas, meeting in an unairconditioned school, the board discussed ways of encouraging men to come to church in short-sleeved shirts without ties. In 1949 this seemed quite radical. When I affirmed the board's intentions and asked what they thought of my doing the same, they indicated clearly that they wanted me to wear jacket and tie! The time lag in ministerial dress is not necessarily caused by clergy. That board may have been saying that the congregation wanted to be led by someone whose dress represented another dimension of worship.

A different garment worn by the leader may actually unite the congregation in worship by means of this difference. The choir may be able to lead the congregation in singing more effectively because they do wear robes. The robes certainly unify the choir itself, and the unit is thereby enabled to lead the congregation in praise. At times choirs have been scattered in the congregation to encourage broader participation. At such a time it is probably better for choir members not to wear robes.

Rituals of worship are effective in part because they follow accepted and reliable ways; however, the vitality of worship can be quickened with new expressions of the old truths. The sermon presents

new combinations of words to create new images of the gospel. They are spoken today and may never be used in this particular way again. In the same way, a minister may put on a garment that expresses some specific idea which, like the grass, grows and withers in a short while. On one occasion the preacher wore a vestment that was made of two vivid color wheels about forty-two inches square. The sermon was aimed at children, but directed to all, saying that the caterpillar must die in order to fly. The message needed the vestment, and the vestment needed the words.

Few churches would have any serious discussion over whether to have the choir in robes, and it is doubtful that a board discussion in a congregation over vestments for the minister would be useful. What is far more important is a relationship between minister and congregation based on a kind of trust that makes it possible to find many ways to communicate the gospel. A minister may wear an alb for the first time and have a white or gold colored stole with symbols of new life on it and announce, "The Lord is risen!" The words and the vestments would be saying the same thing. The quality of trust in the gospel and in one another that pervades a service is what permits people to worship through different vestments. A minister who *imposes* the same vestment on a congregation as if it were *the* way to dress and they had better accept it has not led the congregation; they have been driven.

Vestments for particular times require planning in advance, giving a large number of people an opportunity to participate in planning, designing, and sewing. Weaving, needlecrafts, and other skills are usually found in most congregations, and these arts can help the church at worship. The Seminary Singers of Perkins School of Theology have made their own stoles as individual expressions of faith. These will probably carry their messages to many churches for years to come.

Let each minister and others bring every imagination to work on the message of the vestments while they remember Dr. Russell's words.

Colors

The power of color has been recognized a long time. When the early church began to wear white at funerals it was proclaiming a faith. During the plagues of the Middle Ages, Christians returned to black as the color for mourning—as the non-Christians did—and it was a vivid expression of the Dark Ages. What colors ought the church to use in its worship? Few churches make fixed rules in this regard. Purple has been widely used in penitential seasons, white in festival seasons, red and green in seasons of response. But such a pattern is too fixed. Old Sarum (Salisbury) Cathedral had a great influence on what the Church of England did from its establishment until now. Its usual colors were blue for the seasons of preparation (Advent and Lent), white for the great festivals (Christmas and Easter), and red for the seasons of response (Epiphany and Pentecost).

The use of colors in vestments and all other liturgical art used by the leaders of worship should be chosen to fit in with the colors of the room as well as their traditional and current relation to the message of the worship service. Flowers have long been a means of speaking volumes through color; in a similar way the colors of vestments can be used to brighten and underline the messages of God's good news. Be open to the possibility of using any color and hue to praise God, because there are no fixed rules on colors.

Texture

There are no clear rules about texture either, but the textures of vestments have a message. The quality of the material augments the color. A heavy, rough fabric can express a penitential idea. A natural, brown burlap or other rough material expresses an attitude of discipline and confession more fully than a soft, purple linen cloth. The proclamation of the faith has many facets, and the texture of the vestments can help express the message.

The use of vestments and all liturgical material for worship can become an extravagance that is unfaithful stewardship no matter how wealthy the congregation. The message of vestments must be faithful to the gospel, and that requires that ministers and congregations not spend so much money as to call attention to the financial value of garments. This is such a relative matter as to be difficult to clarify, but it is a matter that cannot be avoided. The status of any church does not need the ostentation of financial opulence. The loving offering of beauty cannot be measured financially. A simple garment cared for and worn with joy speaks in worship a truer message than quantities of gold threads before which the people gasp.

FIVE

Uses of Time

In order to plan and conduct a service of worship it is important to have some awareness of the way in which time is recognized and used. There are many helpful studies that can build a foundation for worship, hence this book will assume that the reader has or can receive knowledge from other sources on how the church has observed time. Certainly the first Christians, who lived in the cycle of the Jewish week and year, had a pattern for the time of their lives. Later, this pattern was seen in a very different light when the followers of Jesus Christ began to live in the expectation of the end of time. A wholly new view of history by a community withdrawing from the world can be seen in the New Testament records. Eschatological concerns could not be preoccupied with calendars and weekly schedules; still, in the earliest records it is clear that new life in the church began to express resurrection faith on the first day of the week, the day of resurrection, the Lord's Day. As the Old Testament went to great lengths to make a case for the Sabbath, so the New Testament presents the case for meeting with the Risen Lord on the first day of the week. By the time Paul wrote to the Corinthians (I Cor. 16:2) the Lord's Day was probably well established.

To plan the service of worship for next Sunday, we must be aware that the Breaking of Bread among Christians in New Testament times had moved through many changes. The devout life of the Jews between Sabbaths placed special ritual emphasis on Monday and Thursday. The first Christians placed their "stations" on Wednesday (the day of betrayal) and Friday (the day of crucifixion) to give a rhythm to the faithful life between the Lord's Days. At first this weekly pattern of life was more important than the annual pattern. In time, both the weekly and the annual cycles became powerful influences on the calendars of Western civilization (Christendom). Our Saturday-Sunday weekends and our Christian holidays are quite influential even in an increasingly secular society.

The monastic orders live out daily and weekly patterns. The full cycle of Psalms each week along with prayers are a framework in which work is done, whereas the secular pattern of the faith requires that prayer and praise be arranged around work schedules. The Christian octave, from Sunday through Sunday, which had resurrection day as its climax, became more dominated by Good Friday when Mass became a daily practice. Paul's emphasis on keeping cross and resurrection as two events of the one great act of redemption was weakened. The Liturgy of the Orthodox Church has retained the resurrection emphasis better than the west has, though life in the Eastern churches gives little evidence of a more joyous faith.

Congregations should be given opportunities to study ways in which Christians have lived out their faith in time. The calendar becomes cluttered, then cleaned; abandoned, then reaccepted. The issues of this book, however, are related to what a congregation might do during and after such a study. In a time when the patterns of Western civilization are gone or going rapidly, what can a community of Christians do to make more fruitful use of time to live out and proclaim the faith? Congregations need to experiment with new patterns of Christian life together.

The Christian year is still a lively option by which faith is celebrated and proclaimed. The broad acceptance of the shape of the year as shown forth in a lectionary is an effective vehicle for giving the gospel a full presentation and enactment. The member churches in the Consultation on Church Union, Roman Catholics, Lutherans, and others, have agreed in large measure on a common lectionary to be read in a three-year cycle. This assumes an agreement on the shape of the year. In this there is a strong affirmation of the central doctrines of the church. The cross/resurrection, the church, the incarnation/manifestation, become central messages based on the historical events which show forth the act of God in Jesus Christ. These and related emphases are a framework by which the church worships God and lives out its faith.

But this is not the only calendar by which the people of our time live. There are national and local calendars, there are agricultural, business, and industrial calendars, and these sociopolitical and economic frameworks manipulate our lives. Twenty-four-hour production schedules, shorter work weeks, and wages are some factors in the social revolution that affect discussions about the Christian week or year. The great economic importance of Christmas has pushed back the number of pre-Christmas shopping days by several weeks. Merchants introduce sights and sounds of Christmas long before the church calendar does, and Christmas Day, which begins a season in the church year, is actually the end of a long, long season in the lives of most church members. The church today has tried to face these calendar changes somewhat by making the first Sunday after Epiphany a celebration of the baptism of Jesus. If Sunday falls on January 6, most modern Christians will be startled to hear of Wise Men so long after the decorations are down and the bowl games are over. The church has also "baptized," or adopted, seasons and holidays which had no special relation to the Christian faith and used these times to celebrate the gospel. That insight ought not to be lost; take New Year's Day, for instance. The ecumenical groups which have worked so well in compiling commonly acceptable lectionaries should continue to work on the church calendar to keep it a means of worship in the midst of changing patterns of the uses of time.

The most important truth about the church year which makes a major difference in the worship services of a congregation is the fact that *the whole gospel* is true every day of the year. The emphases of the doctrines of the church can be proclaimed and celebrated in their fullness as we lift up portions of the whole for special emphasis in particular services. Just as it is a disservice to split cross and resurrection, it is heresy to separate any part of the Christian message from the whole. The way in which the church has isolated itself from the Old Testament is the best illustration of the distortions which appear when the whole message is atomized. Advent is not a season when the people "play like" Jesus has not been born and lived and died and risen. Some remote Sunday after Pentecost is no time to act as if the congregation is "on its own." With an awareness of the whole truth of the faith each Sunday, worship is an opportunity to praise God for all the good news in terms of one particular aspect of it.

If wholeness is the important foundation for the year, it is essential that this wholeness impinge on the life and lives of the congregation now. The exegesis of the biblical record and of tradition cannot be complete until a careful study of the gathered community has been made. Harry Emerson Fosdick's famous words are still needed: "Only the preacher proceeds still upon the idea that folk come to church desperately anxious to discover what happened to Jebusites."[1] This statement is still true fifty years later, but the problems are compounded even more. Nowadays the people don't know what God was doing with the Jebusites and their neighbors, so how can we expect a sermon on their roots to give a better understanding of what God still does with the likes of us? The whole gospel found in the biblical record must reach pew level in the here and now.

The regular weekly service of worship by a congregation of Christians bears a heavy responsibility. First, there is a contract for time. This may sound formal and legalistic, but even when it is not,

the contract is just as definite. Those of us who are
heirs of the union of Sunday and Sabbath laws
looked on the day of rest as a different, though
busy, time. The hours for many church activities
varied, but eleven o'clock in the morning for the
main worship service was invariable. There is no
reason why the eleven o'clock hour should be
changed, but there is every reason why worshipers
should be given wide choices for other times of
worship. A church whose membership is too great
to be seated in the worship room usually has two or
more services on Sunday morning. People who
work on shifts or whose work week gives them
different "weekends" should be given opportunities to meet at convenient times. In areas and
congregations where a significant number of
people own weekend houses, there may be a
week-night service of worship which would be
suitable for them. We know that the patterns of our
lives are changing, and the church must adjust its
schedules to fit the lives of its members. Chris-
tianity speaks to the needs of today or it doesn't
speak at all.

Second, the people of the congregation have a
right to negotiate a contract for the length of the
worship time. This will be set by the customs and
circumstances of the people. Most of the churches
with predominantly black memberships have
services that usually last longer than an hour. Few
of these services will go more than two hours, most
of them will be closer to one and a half hours. The
"established" white services usually last an hour.
In some churches where "revival" patterns govern
most of the orders of worship, services will often

last more than one hour. Few congregations have regular services of worship shorter than one hour. In some churches where several services are conducted on Sunday morning, starting on successive hours, services may last forty-five to fifty minutes. The length of services varies, but every congregation will have a time limit beyond which members will look at their watches and feel it's late. There are rare times when something happens in the service that makes it quite right to go overtime, but the "rightness" should be felt and known by a significant percentage of the people and not just the leader.

Within the limits of a particular service a great deal must be done. In this limited time the church must do so much more than was necessary in a culture dominated by Christendom with its daily services. The Sunday service cannot be directed only to a celebration of the resurrection as if we had moved through the penitential rites of previous services. And just as certainly the time cannot be spent on a "mourners' bench" as if redemption had not come. In other words, the time allotted is *the* time for a representation and reliving of the story of our salvation. We are often reminded that we do not have to re-invent the wheel every time we get into our automobiles, but there are times when we need to be grateful that the wheel *was* invented and that we are responsible for its use. The time for worship becomes a capsule of the Christian life and the leader of the service must act in ways that enable the congregation to *move* through this story. And as it is true with the year, so it is with the hour: The whole gospel is true throughout the hour. How, then, can we make the most of it?

When the shape of the service is determined and its logic clear to the planning team and the leader, it becomes obvious that it is a movement in time. If a basic pattern from *Word and Table* is used, its movement from the gathering of the church through the dismissal will be clear.[2] Get a bulletin and look at a particular service. It is not difficult to find many orders of worship which have a prelude, introit, call to worship, invocation, and opening hymn. Each of these is a "beginning," and this many starts seem more circular than directional. Although this is not to suggest that a service must move in a straight line, like an escalator moving without pause, it is desirable that the order of the worship seem clear and uncluttered to the majority of the congregation. Certainly the leader and those who plan the order of worship ought to have no doubt about its logic. A number of services in United Methodism today reflect real uncertainty about the place of scripture and sermon in relation to each other. The offertory is frequently placed in the service in a location that defies an obvious rationale. The same might be said for the affirmation of faith or creed.

As a service is planned, it is important to realize that people can move from one idea to another quite rapidly. We know more about attention spans today, and those of us who watch television know how long seven minutes can be or how short an hour is. The leader of the service must be fully aware of the order and motion of a particular service, find words and actions which will represent each thrust of the service, and be able to bring the congregation willingly along. A prelude, greeting, call to worship, hymn, and invocation are a cluster of "startings" that may choke the opening minutes of a service.

Because the service must encompass many facets of the gospel, the emphasis of the service determined by the calendar, lectionary, and local situation should be broadly conceived, but specifically expressed. A first hymn of praise to God which opens worshipers to the awesome wonder of God Almighty need not be drawn from the specific message of the scripture lessons which will follow some minutes later. The pattern of the church year is sufficiently well known that congregations expect certain opening hymns on special festival days, yet it is a shame that our well-known Easter hymns cannot be sung on any day—when it is resurrection that calls us to Christian worship any time, any place.

When a particular aspect of God's call to us is reflected in the church calendar and a particular doctrine, the opening hymn and prayers may follow the same general theme. The transition to the service of the Word may move in quite another direction without any great jolt. For instance, the psalm following the absolution in Anglican Morning Prayer is a joyous response to God's pardon which completes one movement but does not introduce the next. A congregation which has completed one act of worship can be led into another rather readily when the leader uses attitude and action to end one phase and move clearly into another. The transitions need not be elaborate but they must be clear—first to the leader, then to the congregation. The movement must not clash, but it does require a willingness to end one act and move directly to another. Some services use the organ to "modulate" from one item to another, but the minds of the congregation are quite able to "change keys" from affirmation to offertory to prayer if the leader moves with clarity and logic.

Bulletins with the order of worship clearly shown are a help to the worshiper. If the acts of worship themselves are not clear, calling a hymn the hymn of dedication will not make it so. A heading about being sent forth into the world is not able to overcome a ceremonial ending that makes one reluctant to leave. The bulletin should provide only the order of a worship service; the acts of worship themselves should be clear enough to need very little commentary in the bulletin.

Worship leaders should anticipate the services they plan to lead until they have already worshiped in them in their imaginations. The parts of the service should be so well rehearsed that the leader can participate fully in and at the same time be alert to small details. Others will be open to the possibility of participation if the leader moves and speaks with certainty. Can you recall the service where the offertory was memorable only because the plates were forgotten, or is a baptism indelibly imprinted on your mind because there was no water in the font? The worship leader is under the demand to participate in the service with the freshness of a new experience and at the same time to have anticipated the whole service as fully as possible.

The clarity of the order in the leader's mind will

also free the leader to meet the unexpected, which may change the timing. Watch a good comedian with skill and practice enough to hold on to some situations or drop a story and go to another depending on the response of the audience. As worship involves more participation by the members of the congregation, the leader must be prepared well enough for the particular service to be able to meet unexpected situations. Suppose the time for congregational concerns gives a person an opportunity to express an idea which elicits wide response from several in the congregation. One who is well prepared for the usual response will be better prepared for the unusual one. It is important to let the member feel free to express the idea. Yet an idea that is widely accepted may call for action and take far more time than allotted. A skilled leader will let the event take place and perhaps shorten or eliminate some of the orders which follow. If it is necessary to go beyond the contracted time, it should be clear from the congregation that to go longer is widely acceptable, and from the leader that those who wish to leave may do so without embarrassment.

A sense of timing is both essential and elusive. The effectiveness of a leader can be measured by her or his sense of timing as much as any other standard. Knowing when to hold on and when to let go requires a feeling for the whole service as well as each component part. It is important to be alert to the reactions of the congregation to what is happening at the moment and also to anticipate the congregation's response to what is to follow. The awkward pause following an act that has finished its course but is not followed by the next act may not be long according to a stopwatch, but it feels interminable to participating worshipers. There may be no such person as a "born leader," but the best leaders seem to have a sense of time that is difficult to teach or learn. There is a rhythm to each worship service which the leader must measure and follow and direct.

The most desirable order of worship gives the congregation an opportunity to celebrate the whole gospel in the accepted length of time. Some clue may be given at the beginning of the service when the people gather to remind them that they are members—they are baptized. A recognition of the call of God and standing at attention before the Lord is a way of starting the service *after* the crossing of the Red Sea or on *this side* of Jordan and Calvary. To recognize ourselves before God and hear the Word of New Life may be well expressed in confession and pardon. Too often our services are judged by their effectiveness in convicting us of sin, and the whole hour can become a time for cutting us down to size. This kind of emphasis is frequently made by those who want to avoid the danger of "cheap grace" at all costs. Then there is the other type of service that tries to be so "positive" that it is equally unrealistic about life. A faithful service of worship will show forth the reality of God as revealed in Jesus Christ. Thanksgiving will be its chief attitude and the people should be able to say a new yes to the Creator's offer of life now. This requires being realistic about sin and salvation. Any service of worship is an opportunity for Christians to give thanks for life up until now and hear the Word and respond to it symbolically and actually in faith and joy. The leader becomes a professional, not in the sense that the service follows a series of knee-jerk exercises disconnected from the soul, but in the sense that it is an authentic expression of the story of our salvation for this day.

With the help of the time of the year and the particular emphasis of the service, members ought to feel they have been moved in time through various aspects of the Christian life as they again affirm their membership, hear the Word of God, respond in gratitude and offering (thanksgiving), each member worshiping in such a way as to be aware of God and others in a new dimension and offering the self to God again in the joyous hope of a transformed life, wherever it is lived and for however long. The leader of the service cannot make this journey for anyone else, but the leader can make this time available so that the gospel might happen again.

SIX

The Work of the People

The person who is the leader of worship represents the church and its faith to the congregation. In all churches which are episcopal, presbyterial, or connectional in any way, the ordained ministry does not hold membership in local congregations. This is an important expression of the catholicity of the church. On the other hand, the minister in charge of a local congregation is also representative of the members of the parish vis-à-vis the whole church. Nowhere else in ministry is this double representation more real than in the worship of the congregation.

The minister of the gospel in the role of worship leader is guiding and enabling persons. There are several criteria by which worship can be judged, but none is more important than broad congregational participation. There are no easy gauges for measuring this participation, but we must be aware that Christian worship is the liturgy of the church, and liturgy is the work of the people—all the people. The liturgical history of the church has often been the record of a lazy membership leaving the work to the ministers in the chancel and of an arrogant ministry decreeing the "right ways" of worship from the chancel and permitting those who would to observe the service.

Broad participation can be increased by enlarging the number of persons who sing in the choirs, who usher, and who assume liturgical responsibilities, such as reading lessons and leading prayers. Without diminishing this kind of participation in the least, there is a need to plan and lead services in such a way as to make each part of the service as broadly available as possible to all the worshipers present.

In this regard, it may be important for us to study the growing practice in many congregations of having a "children's sermon." This is often done by asking the children to come to the chancel and sit on the steps while the minister sits down in a sort of suffer-the-little-children scene to tell a story or bring out an object lesson. After the service some grandparent will tell the minister that the children's sermon was the better of the two. This says at least three important things about the situation: First, any idea that is expressed vividly and briefly is better heard by any age group than a long discussion. Second, taking special notice of children for a few minutes of a service may be shortchanging or exploiting them. Third, and most important, ministers who try to preach children's sermons should study the ways in which children think and assimilate. Child psychologists are in general agreement that children do little abstract thinking before they are about thirteen, so therefore, they do not understand object lessons as adults do.[1] A well-told story will be heard by children with far better comprehension. I conducted a "junior church" for almost a year, and looking back I regret my part in separating families and the way I filled time until I could hear the organ upstairs playing the last hymn. The contemporary children's sermon must be given far more serious preparation and thought in terms of how children hear and understand, or the practice should be abandoned.

Most services have a number of acts which

children ought to be encouraged to know and participate in. When children sit with their parents and siblings, the hymns, responses, Lord's Prayer, and acts of standing, sitting, kneeling, moving, can all be entered into by children from kindergarten age on. American advertisers know how important children are, but a worship service must be directed to a wider audience than the one that watches Saturday morning TV. Moreover, a service of worship includes persons of differing ages and varying backgrounds. A service that ignores children is a poorly planned one if children are present, but it is also poorly planned if any particular age group or type is ignored. Some singles criticize services for being planned as if only family units were present. The worship of the church can be a regular time when we associate with people of all ages instead of an unrealistic, "closely graded" world we ourselves have created.

There are many different churches whose styles of worship vary greatly, and this is valuable in a pluralistic society. It is difficult, however, to envisage a Christian community establishing its chief worship gathering with limits on age, sex, social position, and the like. The people of God gathered for worship should be as broad a representation of God's people as possible.

Each congregation will worship in its own way, and much has been said in this book that encourages congregational identity. There is also a denominational tradition and order which is valuable. Orthodox, Roman Catholics, Lutherans, Anglicans, and others who have rather fixed rituals can be quickly identified in any congregation, but that is certainly not true of United Methodists. There is no mandate to conduct worship in uniform ways, and the varieties are many. *The Book of Hymns* and *The Book of Worship* are official but often not followed. However, these official books and a growing number of supplemental worship resources provided by the Section on Worship are used enough to be a true expression of the connectionalism of United Methodism. It will also be faithful to its tradition by making each service an expression of the Christian faith for each place and time. The major issue in a United Methodist worship service is not its sameness with all others but its faithfulness and vitality in its worship of God. This only suggests some of the dimensions of concern rather than answers to specific questions. The issue of faithful worship which is a vehicle for vital faith is before the church each time it gathers. Some of us who are involved with the worship life of The United Methodist Church often start our work with an emphasis on the forms and orders. It is better to begin with a lively faith which seeks the forms and orders to express that faith. On the other hand, we must remember, as Wesley did, that the orders themselves can be converting.

In a certain small congregation there were several highly educated people with many advanced academic degrees. This was impressive to the young pastor who found helpful and critical support by these people of great significance to him. But in this same church there was also a valuable contribution rendered by an older man who could hardly write his name yet proved to be of immeasurable help to the pastor as one who loved and served God in his own way. The leader of worship ought to know that he or she must work hard to be a good leader for the latter as well as the former. Ministers have often been more conscious of some sorts of persons and have planned for them, ignoring others who need their understanding help just as much.[2]

The leader as a representative person has the dual responsibility of representing not only the gospel and the church, but also the members of the congregation. It is, therefore, highly desirable that the minister know as many of the worshipers as possible. All sorts and conditions of persons will need to be considered in every act of worship. Joining a great parade can be a tremendous act of worship on All Saints' Day, but it cannot be done without considering those who can join only in a nonmarching way.[3] The sensitive leader will find ways to include even those who cannot participate fully. Much more difficult is the way in which persons who do not want to participate are not made to feel manipulated or unnecessarily conspicuous. A service in which the people are given an opportunity to renew their baptism should give those who do not wish to renew an alternative place or act. A sense of community and membership is greatly to be desired in Christian worship, but individuality must also be respected. There are no easy rules for achieving both, but the reality of the work of all the people in the worship of God sets the two foci around which all worship must revolve.

James T. Cleland carried to a logical conclusion what John Knox suggested about the two foci of preaching. Cleland called one focus the Good News and the other the Contemporary Situation. The ellipse which results from the faithful recognition of both foci Cleland calls The Word of God. One can see true liturgy as the ellipse around the reality of God and the expressed faith of the people.[4] The minister who leads a congregation must be aware of the unity of this ellipse and also of the tension within it.

At eye level in front of me is a large copy of Luther's sacristy prayer in translation. The last paragraph just seemed to light up: "Use me as Thy instrument in Thy service. Only do not Thou forsake me, for if I am left to myself, I will certainly bring it all to destruction. Amen." The awareness of what we may do to diminish worship is surpassed only by the faith that God can and does transform our offerings into new life. God can use us as instruments by which the church can worship.

THANKS BE TO GOD.

NOTES

1. The Planning Team

1. *The Book of Worship for Church and Home. With orders of worship, services for the administration of Sacraments, and aids to worship according to the usages of The Methodist Church* (Nashville: The Methodist Publishing House, 1964, 1965).
2. *The Sacrament of the Lord's Supper, An Alternate Text, 1972* (Nashville: The United Methodist Publishing House, 1972).
3. *Word and Table: A Basic Pattern of Sunday Worship for United Methodists* (Nashville: Abingdon, 1976).
4. Music composed in 1969, copyrighted in 1973 by John Erickson.

2. Spoken Words

1. *Proposed. The Book of Common Prayer and Administration of the Sacraments and Other Rites and Ceremonies of the Church Together with the Psalter or Psalms of David According to the use of The Episcopal Church* (New York: The Church Hymnal Corporation and The Seabury Press, 1977), p. 80.
2. *The Book of Common Prayer* with a variety of editions and titles has been one of the most influential books in the English language since Thomas Cranmer produced it in 1549.

3. Ernest Best, *From Text to Sermon: Responsible Use of the New Testament in Preaching* (Atlanta: John Knox Press, 1978), chapter 1.
4. Rober W. Hovda, *Strong, Loving and Wise: Presiding in the Liturgy* (Washington, D.C.: The Liturgical Conference, 1976), p. 48. This book by a Jesuit scholar is of value to all leaders of worship.
5. Frederick Buechner, *Telling the Truth: The Gospel as Tragedy, Comedy and Fairy Tale* (New York: Harper & Row, 1977), pp. 16-17.

4. The Use of Things

1. Gregory Dix, *The Shape of the Liturgy* (London: Dacre Press, Adam and Charles Black, 1945, 1964).
2. Hovda, p. 80.
3. Robert W. Jenson, *Visible Words: The Interpretation and Practice of Christian Sacraments* (Philadelphia: Fortress Press, 1978), p. 69.
4. Christa C. Mayer-Thurman, *Raiment for the Lord's Service: A Thousand Years of Western Vestments* (The Art Institute of Chicago, 1975).

5. Uses of Time

1. Harry Emerson Fosdick, "What Is the Matter with Preaching?" in *Harper's Magazine*, July 1928, p. 135.
2. *Word and Table*, p. 8.

6. The Work of the People

1. Ruth M. Beard, *An Outline of Piaget's Developmental Psychology for Students and Teachers* (New York:

Basic Books, 1969). A helpful study for those who communicate with children in worship.

2. William H. Willimon, *Worship as Pastoral Care* (Nashville: Abingdon, 1979). This is a study of the relationship of the worship leader to the people which deals in depth with this matter.
3. Richard Avery and Donald Marsh, "The Great Parade" (Port Jervis, N.Y.: Proclamation Productions, 1971).
4. John Knox, *The Integrity of Preaching* (Nashville: Abingdon, 1957), p. 22; James T. Cleland, *Preaching to Be Understood* (Nashville: Abingdon, 1965), p. 42 ff.